Machine

IN SEARCH OF MEDIA

Götz Bachmann, Timon Beyes, Mercedes Bunz,
and Wendy Hui Kyong Chun, Series Editors

Machine

**Thomas Pringle, Gertrud Koch,
and Bernard Stiegler**

IN SEARCH OF MEDIA

University of Minnesota Press
Minneapolis
London

meson press

In Search of Media is a collaboration between the
University of Minnesota Press and meson press,
an open access publisher, https://meson.press/.

Every effort was made to obtain permission to reproduce
material in this book. If any proper acknowledgment has not
been included here, we encourage copyright holders to notify
meson press.

Published by the
University of Minnesota Press, 2019
111 Third Avenue South, Suite 290
Minneapolis, MN 55401-2520
https://www.upress.umn.edu

in collaboration with
meson press
Salzstrasse 1
21335 Lüneburg, Germany
https://meson.press

ISBN 978-1-5179-0649-8 (pb)
A Cataloging-in-Publication record for this book is available
from the Library of Congress.

The University of Minnesota is an equal-opportunity educator
and employer.

UMP BmB

Contents

Series Foreword

"Media determine our situation," Friedrich Kittler infamously wrote in his Introduction to *Gramophone, Film, Typewriter.* Although this dictum is certainly extreme—and media archaeology has been critiqued for being overly dramatic and focused on technological developments—it propels us to keep thinking about media as setting the terms for which we live, socialize, communicate, organize, do scholarship, et cetera. After all, as Kittler continued in his opening statement almost thirty years ago, our situation, "in spite or because" of media, "deserves a description." What, then, are the terms—the limits, the conditions, the periods, the relations, the phrases—of media? And, what is the relationship between these terms and determination? This book series, *In Search of Media,* answers these questions by investigating the often elliptical "terms of media" under which users operate. That is, rather than produce a series of explanatory keyword-based texts to describe media practices, the goal is to understand the conditions (the "terms") under which media is produced, as well as the ways in which media impacts and changes these terms.

Clearly, the rise of search engines has fostered the proliferation and predominance of keywords and terms. At the same time, it has changed the very nature of keywords, since now any word and pattern can become "key." Even further, it has transformed the very process of learning, since search presumes that, (a) with the right phrase, any question can be answered and (b) that the answers lie within the database. The truth, in other words, is "in there." The impact of search/media on knowledge, however, goes beyond search engines. Increasingly, disciplines—from sociology to economics, from the arts to literature—are in search of media as a way to revitalize their methods and objects of study. Our current media situation therefore seems to imply a new term, understood as temporal shifts of mediatic conditioning. Most broadly, then, this series asks: What are the terms or conditions of knowledge itself?

To answer this question, each book features interventions by two (or more) authors, whose approach to a term—to begin with: *communication, pattern discrimination, markets, remain, machine*— diverge and converge in surprising ways. By pairing up scholars from North America and Europe, this series also advances media theory by obviating the proverbial "ten year gap" that exists across language barriers due to the vagaries of translation and local academic customs. The series aims to provoke new descriptions, prescriptions, and hypotheses—to rethink and reimagine what media can and must do.

Un/Civil Engineering
Thomas Pringle

In Ted Chiang's (2002) sci-fi short story "Seventy-Two Letters," the young protagonist uses epithetical codes to program the behavior of golem-like autonomous robots against the backdrop of a speculative nineteenth-century England. Upon discovering an epithet that allows the construction of automata capable of building other simple automata, the Industrial Revolution–esque society is thrown into a crisis. While the character's discovery is intended to release proletariat laborers from horrid factory conditions through the automated production of inexpensive machine engines that could potentially regrow the cottage industries lost to manufactories, the prospect of true self-reproducing machines unintentionally draws the ire of a powerful union of sculptors tasked with handcrafting the automata. The threat of reproductive machines is a contradiction, insofar as the laborers carefully sculpting the automata—with prestige and by hand—reject a technological development that promises to reinstate their own preferred labor conditions to the oppressed and demeaned textile workers. Referencing the Goethe poem "The Sorcerer's Apprentice" in support of their cause, the unionists recount the cautionary tale of the self-generating anthropomorphic brooms whose simple machinic function to fill buckets of water and clean the floor turns into an out-of-control mess.

The story's protagonist rejects the warning that automata could self-reproduce without human assistance as an outdated objection and insists that there remains a radical political potential for new democratic machines working alongside laboring people. Goethe's account of automated destruction and an assistant pleading the sorcerer to rescue a situation run amok is a widely applied cliché, but Chiang's political setting offers insight for how the perception of machines as objects of work, beauty, knowledge, and play remains a societal problem. The machine could be a savior to some and a curse for others, and, either way, its mass manufacture promises to recast the social fabric at large. Today, the question is less about the dangers of total mechanization—the nightmare prediction of science fiction and antihumanism—or the operation of systems without adequate knowledge or experience, as access to technology is diffractively policed according to the persisting human assumptions of discrimination and hierarchy that machines working under capitalism tend to reproduce and reinforce. Instead, having accepted machines as ubiquitous, helpful, and necessary elements of society, the question becomes, How does machine implementation mean a vastly different promise to different collectives of people? Is the world of the engineer the same as the laborer, the same as the machine? With what framework do we describe our affinities with and hatreds of machines, as we so often learn from their vision?

In a political climate where machines operate pervasively and abundantly, on great and small scales, the precise role of human beings as operators, users, or conductors and the according social formations of humans alongside machines remain unresolved. The ideological messianism of social network politics, the belief in the powers of Big Data, the governance of algorithms, those individual habits formed alongside mass-produced devices, or the materiality and unequal availability of technological infrastructure—each scenario is politically familiar yet demands a new critique that distills how individuals have become reticulated as collectives within a thoroughly technologized landscape. Then, machines at scale both offer and demand a kind of social thinking about collectives of people and technology that operate seen and unseen, unconsciously embodied and actively felt. The mass-produced, large- or micro-scale machine forces us to intersect and replace categories of social analysis that relate the individual to familiar groupings—like the subject to the nation—with novel modes of thinking across the singular and plural. For example, is "nationalist fervor" an appropriate description for those numerous Apple fans excited by the release of a new iPhone? How are biometric databases and technologies at once detecting and creating collectives, and are these machines useful, safeguarding, or simply discriminatory? What are "circadian rhythms" in a world with high-frequency trading, the uniformity of Google Spanner, Runtastic's development of an iPhone app for dream betterment, or Netflix's venture into wearable technology that pauses your film when you fall asleep? What is labor when factories are mobile, prefabricated, and autonomous or when social networks mine the reticulated composition of human relationships for value? Critical inquiry into machines operating at speed and scale is increasingly necessary, *as not all engineers are civil.*

Taking up this project from different perspectives, this book questions the contemporary status of the machine as a political configuration of the individual to the technical and the collective. Focusing on "animate," Gertrud Koch looks at the pathological relationships that develop between people and technology. Questioning an ontological distinction between humans and machines, she locates the contemporary practice of "performance capture" in film within a longer technological history describing the technical connections interfacing humans and machines as ontologically operative. By turning from technological distinction to functionality, the technical animation of the world is tied to a dynamic development of the human. Conceptually, Koch frames the animating human as a formal medium of perception achieved through a polyvalent interchange found in the relation between the personal use of machines and the natural surface of the world that technological thinking surfaces as axiomatic. This, however, leaves an open question: what is the role of beauty in the function of a machine?

In his articulation of an "automatic society," Bernard Stiegler discerns a governance of "hypercontrol" that follows from the historical installment of digital media networks. In place of functions previously tackled by the mind, the processes of mathematical automation that are externalized in digital technology operate without human direction and oversight. This externalization of formerly internal cognitive operations supplements the thought of large populations by automatically rendering each user as an individual and collective at once, through shared psychical experience mediated by social technology. Within this singular yet interlaced vision of society, for Stiegler, is a new proletariat of knowledge workers who are mnemotechnically captured and industrially automated. According to this paradigm of intellectual and informational capital, there are new arrangements of conceptual production that are consequential symptoms of an automatic society: the Anthropocene and Chris Anderson's "The End of Theory." Yet, there is also a latent cure, as Stiegler posits the internet as a possibly redemptive *pharmakon.* Closing with a meditation on the potential for reclaiming human agency, he describes a substitutional paradigm of a "negentropic" society that would hold the potential to release network culture from its automatic force.

Thomas Pringle describes the history of the "ecosystem" as a machinic term that allows conceptual traffic between the study of ecology and economy. Set against the background of twentieth-century technoscience, the ecosystem takes on a new political valence given its operation in resource management, national security, and environmental economic planning. Tracing the term alongside theoretical efforts to describe the operation of power as an ecology composed between the poles of mind, technology, and environment, he resolves in a sustained engagement with how the term resurfaces organicist social orientations. Most recently, this vitalism and its relationship to political economy take the form of "resilience": a policy discourse developed from the ecosystem that seeks to strategically adapt finances and security to conditions of ecological turbulence and disequilibrium.

In each case, the author sees room for *machine*—or its animating/ automating qualities—to operate as a term of media analysis giving specific attention to contemporary technosocial politics. Each author carefully avoids the pitfalls of Promethean, techno-utopian, and technological determinist perspectives in favor of positions that balance the machine on a finely nuanced line between the singular and the plural, the ideological and the scientific, the technological and the functional. While machines do hold the power to capture individuals, the authors seek critical positions from which the agency of the human is not dismissed in advance and life alongside technology can be repaired. However, a central problem and difference between entries remain in the degree to which each critic seeks to gain distance from, or proximity to, the technologies under analysis, as machines inevitably place pressure on the production of theoretical knowledge. With this reflexive notice in mind, perhaps it's best to begin with pragmatic words of advice from the engineer that could be useful for any future sorcerer's apprentice: to understand recursion, one must first understand recursion.

Reference

Chiang, Ted. 2002. "Seventy-Two Letters." In *Stories of Your Life and Others,* 147–200. New York: Tor.

Animation of the Technical and the Quest for Beauty

Gertrud Koch

The Human Body as Generic Form:
On Anthropomorphism in Media

In the Aristotelian view of the generic, *species* is defined as a distinct, classificatory term, while *generic form* is distinguished as a "preliminary step" to a "specific form." This includes, for instance, the "perceptive faculty" as a "generic form" of human beings. It makes us into the tasting, smelling, hearing, seeing, and feeling beings that are generated in these perceptions, without this already being sufficient to define us as members of a specific species.

The perceptive faculty as a generic form of the human being would therefore be what links humans with other animals, a common form of being-in-the-world as a concrete body. But we can also describe the difference between the various forms of living beings with regard to their differently developed capacities. The generic form of the perceptive faculty can link an octopus with a human being without having to subsume the two under the same developmental tendency. In this respect, generic forms are nonteleological. If we start from this model, then we can conceive of further generic forms of perception, such as perspective or the ability to distinguish being light and shadow. The latter allows us to see shadows *as images,* unrelated to whether we can also *feel* them in the warm–cold distinction. The shadow itself can also be regarded as a further generic form that allows for various other distinctions. It can be viewed as an image, as a spectacle of nature, as a shadow play converted into a fixed form with rules, as artificial play, and so on. Film, for example, can make use of both varieties of the shadow in its aesthetic operations. This need not imply the emergence of lower and higher forms of the shadow—or that film has a greater capacity to exhaust the generic form of the shadow.

What might the term *generic form* explain? It can be distinguished from other terms like *open form* or *operation.* While the *open form* is a definition of form that refers to its semantic unfinished quality, the *operation* is defined in terms of its production aesthetics, that is, pragmatically, referring in its aesthetics to the artistic act. In contrast, we should use *generic form* to designate the initiating function of *particular* perceptions, which are neither random (we cannot see everything, but only in perspectival scales, for instance, no shadows without light) nor obligatory (in a three-dimensional space with light and shadow, for instance, I can only have "eyes" for a graphic ground pattern or mainly sense cold). These generic forms of the perceptive faculty turn from the sensory to the aesthetic when they apply perceptions as accentuations that simultaneously take recourse in the world of the perceptible while fictionalizing it (*x* emerges from the shadows) or instilling it with imaginative qualities ("faces in the cloud,"[1] etc.).

If we understand generic forms in this sense, as formative forms that nonteleologically unfold toward a final stage, which characterizes a fluid dynamic of forms, this would then imply revising the ontological status of forms. For forms that unfold teleologically strive for an end point that can be explicitly defined. If we abandon this idea, then we also must define a new understanding of ontology in the context of the term *generic form,* one that includes the operative aspects that precede semantization.

In the following, I view the human body as a medium of the human "perceptive faculty" under the dual aspect of the generic form and operative ontology—behind this concept are concepts and ideas from the philosophies of media, technology, and culture that attempt to reconceive the relationship between nature–culture–human and technology. The human perceptive faculty, however, not only differs from that of the octopus in purely biological terms, for instance, but also because of its relations. The human perceptive faculty is not only directed at our natural surroundings but also itself makes use of all kinds of machines, apparatuses, and technologies that, roughly speaking, operatively define what human beings are, in and through our perceptive faculty, in relation to the world of technology as much as to our "natural" biological configuration.

In many discourses, these areas where human beings and machines are linked become made into binary odd couples. Wherever there is technology, the grass of nature can no longer grow; where there is culture, we are alienated from nature; wherever nature exists, culture stops; under the sign of the age of technology arises a technocracy, the dominance of technical-calculating functional thinking, which suffocates the organically grown living world in the chilling grasp of functional administrative rationality, banishing the individual to that "shell of bondage" *(stahlharte Gehäuse der Hörigkeit)* evoked by Max Weber. In his writings in *Economy and Society,* Weber (1978, 1402) introduces the machine metaphor in a double pack when he writes,

> An inanimate machine is mind objectified. Only this provides it with the power to force men into its service and to dominate their everyday working life so completely as is actually the case in the factory. Objectified intelligence is also that animated machine, the bureaucratic organization, with its specialization of trained skills, its division of jurisdiction, its rules and hierarchical relations of authority. Together with the inanimate machine it is busy fabricating the shell of bondage which men will perhaps be forced to inhabit some day, as powerless as the fellahs

of ancient Egypt. This might happen if a technically supe-
rior administration were to be the ultimate and sole value
in the ordering of their affairs, and that means: a rational
bureaucratic administration with the corresponding wel-
fare benefits, for this bureaucracy can accomplish much
better than any other structure of domination.

The inanimate and the animate machine together produce that
Procrustean bed on which each individual is held and threatened
to tear that individual apart. The prognostic vision of the bourgeois
individual, who in the end is swallowed by the apparatus of domination, much like the Egyptian fellahs were with enslavement by
the machine, belongs to the ironclad stock of cultural and social
theory in which the "machine"—the "apparatus"—is conceived
in opposition to the individual. Whether it is precisely the "spirit
of Protestantism" that "is objectified" in the doubled machine of
technological production and administrative state will here be left
to Max Weber studies and to the history of religion. What continues to be in effect to this day is Weber's thesis of rationalization,
regardless of any individual objections—even if it has often been
reduced and battered into cultural-critical formulas that can no
longer maintain the vehemence of Weber's thesis.

These litanies are long and familiar. In them the complex architecture of modern society is reduced to an apocalyptic power struggle
between distinct camps and parties—and the osmotic connections
between the areas are no longer perceived or are only helplessly
experienced as impenetrable brush. Machines are then assessed
to be overpowering and headstrong, without being able or even
wanting to separate ourselves from them.

But kicking the car, patting the closed computer laptop, wildly
pressing random keys, or frantically calling out hello into your
malfunctioning iPhone—these minor pathologies of everyday life
and their outbursts of irrational behavior tell a different story: the
rocky relationship in which humans and machines are stuck. If we
follow the symptoms, then we see that it comes down to problems

of living together, or trouble in the relationship. At least the pathological kick to the machine knows that it is entering into a relationship with the machine, even if it is a negative and destructive one.
And yet, our pathological relationship to the machine points to an
affective knowledge that acknowledges mutual interdependence.
The machine wants to be used correctly, carefully installed and
maintained, and understood in its abilities. If these conditions are
not fulfilled and the interplay with the machine is troubled, the
relationship to the machine is negative. The possibility of imagining
our relation to technology as a relationship that we have with
machines has been compared with the work of a conductor by
the French psychologist and philosopher Gilbert Simondon (2017,
17–18):

> Far from being the supervisor of a group of slaves, man is
> the permanent organizer of a society of technical objects
> that need him in the same way musicians in an orches-
> tra need a conductor. The conductor can only direct the
> musicians because he plays the piece in the same way
> they do, as intensely as they all do; he tempers or hurries
> them, but is also tempered or hurried by them; in fact, it
> is through the conductor that the members of the orches-
> tra temper or hurry one another, he is the moving and
> current form of the group as it exists for each of them;
> he is the mutual interpreter of all of them in relation to
> one another. Man thus has the function of being the per-
> manent coordinator and inventor of the machines that
> surround him. He is *among* the machines that operate
> with him.

Simondon recommends a different way of dealing with machines,
which are not our externalizable Other or beings from another
world that have occupied our own, but which exist with us in a
single world, which belong to us, and which define us in the way we
define and view them as belonging to us. Simondon substantiates
this relationship with a further metaphor in which he sees us as
"translating between the machines." This unavoidable dynamic in

the relationship between human being and machine makes any strict ontological distinction between us impossible, for the way technological objects exist is not related to any other world, as we define ourselves with and through machines: there are operative ontologies that are produced and altered in our practical dealings with machines.

It is uncontested that our natural faculties have not essentially changed in evolutionary terms since the beginning of the species, and yet by now we can do certain things as a species that we learned through our interactions with machines. For instance, our ways of traveling have expanded since we learned to walk upright. We can now also move across long stretches in the air or over water; we can wash our blood with the aid of machines and attach an iron lung to breathe with. Using optical aids, we can see from all sides, look around the corner, see in the dark, and so on. This means that we invent technological objects that constantly alter our anthropological conditions and thus human ontology and the way human beings exist. By assuming this position, cultural technologies could be defined as practices of dealing with technological objects and artifacts of all kinds, which constantly reframe our understanding of ourselves. This is the sense in which Weber (1978, 65) also regarded the term *technology* as a term of action when he wrote,

> The "technique" of an action refers to the means employed as *opposed* to the meaning or end to which the action is, in the last analysis, oriented. "Rational" technique is a choice of means which is consciously and systematically oriented to the experience and reflection of the actor, which consists, at the highest level of rationality, in scientific knowledge. What is concretely to be treated as a "technique" is thus variable. The ultimate meaning of a *concrete* act may, seen in the *total* context of action, be of a "technical" order; that is, it may be significant only as a means in this broader context. Then the "meaning" of the *concrete* act (viewed from the larger context) lies in its

technical function; and conversely, the means which are applied in order to accomplish this are its "techniques." In this sense there are techniques of every conceivable type of action, techniques of prayer, of asceticism, of thought and research, of memorizing, or education, or exercising political or hierocractic domination, of administration, of making love, of making war, of musical performances, of sculpture and painting, or arriving at legal decisions. All of these are capable of the widest variation in degree of rationality.

"What is concretely to be treated as a 'technique' is thus variable," writes Weber (65). Techniques are therefore instances of an action that are part of a wider context into which they merge. Machines can become part of techniques, for instance, of traveling, of writing down, of transmitting sound and light waves, which would make them media that performatively intervene in our action by facilitating or torpedoing certain techniques. In this respect, there is a paradigm change: machines are no longer extensions of organs, as older anthropologists thought (Arnold Gehlen, etc.), but agents in a field of techniques and part of a network of relations. And often enough, they are a pathologically distorted relation: the fact that worn-out goods take their toll on us every day—for instance, when an easily broken handle puts an otherwise usable machine out of service—points to economic calculations already in a machine's production that convert its function from mechanical-technical to economic. Here as well, the technological malfunction of the machine indicates a disturbance in the social relationship to it and its users. In such a pragmatic reading, the demonization of the machine would vanish as much as would the fetishization that sticks to it in its form as commodity.

Being inventive in our dealings with machines, which we find so difficult in our everyday lives, since it is often already foreclosed in production, marks the aesthetic relationship to the machine and, according to Weber (1978, 67), is fundamental to the emergence of technology, for the fact that what is called the technological development of modern times has been so largely oriented economically to profit-making is one of the fundamental facts of the history of technology. But however fundamental it has been, this economic orientation has by no means stood alone in shaping the development of technology. In addition, a part has been played by the games and cogitations of impractical ideologists, a part by other-worldly interests and all sorts of fantasies, a part by preoccupation with artistic problems, and by various other non-economic motives.

If we read this passage with Simondon in mind, then we notice that there is a technological reference back to art and game, in Weber as a historical source, in Simondon in the metaphor of the conductor. In the following, I would now like to use two examples in an attempt to show how the human body as a medium of the generic form "perceptive faculty," becomes activated in the field of aesthetic objects, thus shifting the ontological definitions of the form "human being." Second, I would like to use the examples to show paradigmatically how the ontology of man and machine operatively relates the one to the other in our technological dealings with machines, thus bringing a kind of fluidity to both rigid ontologies, which operate with a logic of subsumption. The "perceptive faculty," as a generic form of the human being, is then itself displaced into an interplay between perception of the self and of the (surrounding) world. The "perceptive faculty" of machines becomes perceptible in the playful interaction with their "conductor," thus becoming aestheticized and thematized as aesthetic objects.

A Case Study: Why Should Andy Serkis
Get an Oscar?

Andy Serkis is a British theater and film actor, known above all for his roles that present purely cinematographic beings—fictional characters that can no longer be cloaked in the corporeal shell of an actor but are new hybrid creations consisting of an interplay

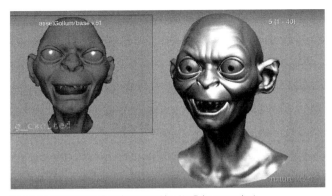

[Figure 1.1.] "Creating Gollum" by naturevideo (YouTube screenshot).

between the human capacities to move, perform, and express with computer-generated image production. Concretely, this means that we as spectators see and hear Andy Serkis in the role of the giant ape King Kong in the film of the same name, as Gollum (from the Lord of the Rings film trilogy [2001–3] and *The Hobbit: An Unexpected Journey* [2012]), as an insurgent ape in the Planet of the Apes film series, and yet we do not see and hear Serkis in the same way that we see him as Othello on stage in Great Britain or in live-action films in his physical form. What appears before us is the result of complex interaction of man, machine, and technology. The production of the Gollum figure shows how the process of becoming a character in a fantasy film develops as the interplay of a theatrical performance and mechanical transmissions technology, which transfers the gestures, facial expressions, and body movements of the actor to machines as material references so that these can be used to create a morphological shaping of computer-generated images. The process is called *performance capture* and is a further development of *motion capture.*

The "technical" advance made between the two films lies in an improvement in plasticity and in the character's carnality, applied by means of digital makeup, muscles, and layers of skin, all oriented

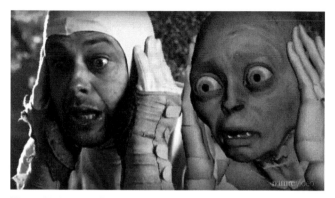

[Figure 1.2.] "Creating Gollum" by naturevideo (YouTube screenshot).

to the physical qualities of the human body and thus representing the attempt to get fantasy artifacts to appear as muscled bodies, speaking with a human voice. The movements and the "carnality" of the computer-generated bodies create the allusion to human bodies and arise as a mimesis of them. The melding of live-action film (filmed with actors on location) and the animated world of special effects dissolves the boundaries of space, thus creating a permanent change in the ontology of what is seen as human or as a human environment. In the end, it is the fusion of the physical body with the machine-generated one that seems to claim that the humanity of human beings is not found in its proximity to nature but in their interaction with the machine, which produces a new idea of the image of the human being that both arises out of its creative cohabitation with machines and reflects on this as well.

When the live-action actor James Franco, who is Andy Serkis's colleague in the film *Rise of the Planet of the Apes* (2011), claims that Serkis deserves an Oscar for his portrayal of the ape Caesar, the provocation lies in how, for the first time, recognition is being demanded for the fact that the creation of an animated character is not solely due to the work of machines and their technical custodians but lives from a mimesis that is at least double: that of an

[Figure 1.3.] *"Rise of the Planet of the Apes* Featurette" by Weta Digital (YouTube screenshot).

actor with regard to the fiction (the role) and that of the machine with regard to the actor. This has changed the discourse. We like to separate live-action film from computer-generated film in terms of their ontology, which is why Oscars are given *either* to actors *or* to technicians, or sometimes to whole studios specialized in special effects, although techniques have long since been formed in the practical use of machines that have this fusion as their goal.

This was James Franco's (2012) plea, who played the scientist as live action opposite Andy Serkis in his role as the insurgent ape Caesar:

> Andy doesn't need me to tell him he is an innovator,
> he knows it. What is needed is recognition for him,
> now. Not later when this kind of acting is *de rigueur,* but
> now, when he has elevated this fresh mode of acting into
> an art form. And it is time for actors to give credit to other
> actors. It is easy to praise the technical achievements of
> this film, but those achievements would be empty with-
> out Andy. Caesar is not a character that is dependent on
> human forms of expression to deliver the emotion of the
> character: despite the lack of any human gestures, and
> maybe two or three words of human speech Caesar is a

fully realized character, not human, and not quite ape; this is no Lassie and this is no Roger Rabbit, it is the creation of an actor doing something that I dare say no other actor could have done at this moment.

And he could only do it by interacting with the machine, which is also neither ape nor human being but a technological object that interacts with us. In this interaction, the old questions of ontology are operatively re-posed: animal, human, machine enter into mimetic exchange processes. Just like the meowing of the cat, which is quiet "by nature," is mimesis of human language, the computer-supported image of the human being is mimesis of both the machine and the human being. We would like to know more about both human and machine, for we already don't know anymore and probably will never be able to know what they are, but we can observe and analyze and try to capture conceptually what they are like.

It was not strictly necessary to propose my outline here as some special case of the cinematographic, such as performance capture. I could also have taken recourse in the "old" unresolved cases, for instance, in films by the silent film comedian Buster Keaton, who was one of the first to take the role of conductor, which I have cited from Simondon, and turn it into a poetics of the slapstick film of technical objects. Not only because he, as film director, is embodied as a performer by the machines of the cinema (above all the camera) but because, in addition, he transforms this relationship between man and machine in the events that occur on the film screen into an aesthetic way of existing, which he produces by combining human and mechanical bodies as an ingenious dance. Or I could refer to the video works of Bill Viola (1986), who carries out a complex visual work on human and animal gazes by reflecting himself toward the camera in the eye of a bird in his work *I Do Not Know What It Is I Am Like* (1986).

On the surface, we see the reflection of the cameraman on the bird's pupil as it looks directly into the camera. But the images

[Figure 1.4.] *I Do Not Know What It Is I Am Like* by Bill Viola (film screenshot).

made possible by the technical processes of digitization are also reflections of the self—a self-portrait of the artist—who responds to the animal's gaze with a projection of his own image. He thus presents himself along with a machine, without which this self-portrait would not be possible. Indeed, the self-portrait is presented with the digital camera, which we see along with him as a symbiotic unity in the self-portrait on the bird's pupil, but also in those shots that divide the video's chapters and show Bill Viola at his electronic editing table and computer, where the video is made.

In his writings, Viola himself refers to video and computer technology as a way to enable the further development of the self and of self-understanding. Viola insists on using the latest machines and software because they stem from the dynamic interaction of man and machine and therefore belong to the generic form of the "perceptive faculty." "The level of use of the tools is a direct reflection of the level of the user. Chopsticks can either be a simple eating utensil or a deadly weapon, depending on who uses them" (Viola, quoted in Perloff 1998, 320). Marjorie Perloff correctly uses this citation to point to the pragmatic side in Viola and to define his poetics. Above all, it is in video technology's provenance from live broadcasting, even before video had been developed as a recording medium, that Viola justifies its greater proximity to the living. In "Between How and Why," Viola (1995, 62–63) writes,

> One of the most fascinating aspects of video's technical evolution, and the one that makes it most different from film, is that the video image existed for many years before a way was developed to record it. . . . Taping or recording is not an integral part of the system. Film is not film unless it is filming (recording). Video, however, is "videoing" all the time, continually in motion, putting out 30 frames, or images, a second. . . . *Video's roots in the live, not recorded, is the underlying characteristic of the medium.* . . . When one makes a videotape, one is interfering with an ongoing process, the scanning of the camera. . . . In film . . . the basic illusion is of movement, produced by the succession of still images flashing on the screen. In video, stillness is the basic illusion: a still image does not exist because the video signal is in constant motion scanning across the screen.

Viola's self-portrait in *I Do Not Know What It Is I Am Like* was literally created as the interface of a machine, the digital camera, video technology, and Viola's work at the computer. The *technē* is his art—the art of recognizing oneself in the mirror—which the machine provides for him, becoming a surface in nature on which to project. Although Viola may see his relationship to nature differently, he brings forth an image as a physical object in the triangulation of man–machine–animal that comes from fusing three bodies and which yields an image of that fusion.

Perloff (1998, 321) concludes her essay with the words "artists like Viola are rediscovering the function of art as a form of practical knowledge—in Plato's words in the *Ion, techne kai episteme.*" And so I would like to conclude this case study, not by turning to

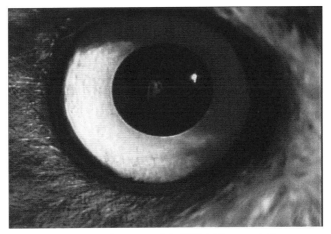

[Figure 1.5.] *I Do Not Know What It Is I Am Like* by Bill Viola (film screenshot).

Platonism, against which the concept of "operative ontology" and of "generic form" are in fact aimed, but by stressing the contents of the formula *technē kai epistēmē,* which does not define art/technologies as the other of awareness but as a connection. Technologies are practical knowledge that we fabricate by dealing with machines. The human body functions in this as a medium that takes on the "generic form of the perceptive faculty."

Beauty and Technology: The Aesthetic Question of Technical Objects

The relationship between art and technology has a long conceptual history that focuses primarily on the technical aspects of production, emphasizing the experimental character of both. [2] Often art is defined as technical itself in the sense of *technē*—or as negation of the instrumental character of technical functionalism by emphasizing the aspect of play. Both definitions fail to grasp the dialectic that spans between the two terms of *art* and *technology.* Art produces in its techniques something immaterial; the beautiful appearance—houses one can't live in, spatial images one can't step in, irons one can't iron with, fires one can't extinguish, dead one can't bury, bursts of violence one can't stop or share. In art's aesthetic operations, all things natural or artificial can become material, and despite its function, art energizes its own transformation into something "beautiful" following the modi of sensual perception. The binary opposition of beautiful–ugly shrinks: even the ugly, the bitter, the painful, gains in its aesthetic appearance an affect of a second order, such as pleasure in horror or lust for disgust.

The Beautiful and the Fetish

The beautiful appearance becomes, in these aesthetic operations of making, an excess that changes functional objects into art objects. The beautiful appearance produces a surplus value: to function beauty adds value to the object. This value has an economic determination: now the technical object is not only practical but also beautiful. That's why Apple products are more expensive than other electronic objects of the same functional type. This economic theory formulates beauty as a "shine" that makes objects appear as something precious and considers the beautiful as a function of the "shine." It produces an enchantment, as though a kind of white magic, that makes the beautiful into a fetish in the same sense as Karl Marx argued in his influential chapter on the fetish character of commodity. Marx argued that the fetish emerges where the commodity is no longer seen as produced by invested labor but only mediated by its price.

I recall a curious example in which something inaccessibly expensive appears as a beautiful object of desire: like everywhere in the globalized media world, game shows run on all channels in the People's Republic of China. These shows often ask the participants to do humiliating things that leave them as losers at the end. The nonsense of play differs nevertheless from these games insofar as there is a winner at the end and there is a material object that can be won—the competition aims for a commodity of high value, or sometimes blunt cash. Humiliation comes as the price to possibly attain something that one couldn't afford otherwise—one could argue that there is a moment of corruption or prostitution involved as a price is paid in order to exhibit someone's lust for an object of desire. In one of these shows, the main prize was a big BMW limousine—a status symbol of the new rich class in China—and in the preparation for the contest, a young female worker was asked why she volunteers for such an endeavor that would probably harm her. Her equally stupefying and illuminating answer was "I'd rather cry in a BMW than smile on a bike."[3]

One can read this sybillinic answer as pointing to the privilege of the well-heeled, as to be unhappy behind the closed curtains of their fancy limousines contrasts with the poor bicyclists who have no chance for a private moment and must show a public smile. But one can also read this anecdote as intensification of the melancholic state that comes with the twisted desires that the commodity fetish evokes—the spell over labor as a precondition of the artifact and the worker that can't reach his work becoming melancholic. The fetish character of the commodity is based on the repression of its material foundation in labor and machinery. Like how the fetish in magical practice operates on the paradox that it is at the same time self-made and fabricated but also entails external magic animated power, the commodity becomes fetish insofar as it appears to those who fabricated it as something magical.

Walter Benjamin (1999, 10) described this relationship as the becoming-image of the commodity:

> But precisely modernity is always citing primal history. Here, this occurs through the ambiguity peculiar to the social relations and products of this epoch. Ambiguity is the appearance of dialectic in images, the law of dialectics at a standstill. This standstill is utopia and the dialectical image, therefore, dream image. Such an image is afforded by the commodity per se: as fetish.

To cry in a BMW, within property that still doesn't gain a concrete value, is a BMW at standstill. Having the BMW will not change the life conditions of a worker into one of the elite, as even the use-value of the limousine may be limited in the hands of a worker who has neither the time nor the means to enjoy such an item. Insofar as the fetish shrinks back into the abstract exchange-value in the medium of money, the end of the dream—or only as a dream image—is the fetish as a sign of happiness. The happiness of uselessness is the possession of a beautiful limousine that doesn't necessarily entail any use as technical object.

A modern aesthetic that poses the question about the value of art draws itself into the paradoxes between two concepts of value. Benjamin brings this question to the table in a quote he takes from Adorno. Benjamin (1999, 669–70), in his notes for the Passagen-Werk, quotes Adorno's essay "Fragments on Wagner" from 1939 with a significant reflection on this relationship:

> The art of Wagner's orchestration has banished . . . the role of the immediate production of sound from the aesthetic totality. . . . Anyone fully able to grasp why Haydn doubles the violins with a flute in piano might get an intuitive glimpse into why, thousands of years ago, men gave up eating uncooked grain and began to bake bread, or why they started to smooth and polish their tools. All trace of its own production should ideally disappear from the object of consumption. It should look as though it had never been made, so as not to reveal that the one who sells it did not in fact make it, but rather appropriated to himself the labor that went into it. The autonomy of art has its origin in the concealment of labor.

Adorno states a dialectical relation between compulsory labor that is necessary to sustain our lives, or the appropriation of labor via the market, and the free work of art that remains illusionary in sheer "shine," but by shining, it indirectly points to its repressed basis. Benjamin cites Adorno within the framework of his own occupation with Marx's idea of commodity fetishism, where he looks at the commodities in the Parisian passages as surrealistic emanations—or one could say Benjamin looks at them as if they were works of art detached from the traces of labor. He reactivates Marx's (1906) famous discussion in *Capital* about the fetish character of the commodity, as Marx claims:

> There it is a definite social relation between men, that assumes, in their eyes, the fantastic form of a relation between things. In order, therefore, to find an analogy, we must have recourse to the mist-enveloped regions of the religious world. In that world the productions of the human brain appear as independent beings endowed with life, and entering into relation both with one another and the human race. So it is in the world of commodities with the products of men's hands. This I call the Fetishism which attaches itself to the products of labour, so soon as they are produced as commodities, and which is therefore inseparable from the production of commodities. (83)

Adorno's conclusion that autonomous art has at its origin the blurring of labor is not only illuminating regarding the reception of Marx in the first generation of the Frankfurt school but astonishing insofar that it discovers aesthetic potential in the few pages of Marx's fetish chapter. Adorno leads us to a complex grid in which the relation between bodily work, technical production, and the autonomous appearance of aesthetic objects are embedded. His look at the value of art through the economic value of production is enlightening for the materialist grounding of art in a praxis of technical fabrication and work. Autonomy becomes a fragile state as it only unfolds as appearance. Insofar as art takes part in the production of the illusion of a work-free realm of commodities, it is negated at the same time through a delusive character by claiming nothing more than just the "shine." Aesthetic illusion turns into the opponent of the delusive character of commodity production.

The Beautiful in the Technical

In his book *The Mode of Existence of Technical Objects,* Gilbert Simondon (2017, 196) dedicates a small chapter to the correlation between technical and aesthetic thinking. Among others, he asks the question, When are technical objects beautiful? First, he refers to those objects that are aesthetically vested in a manner that hides their technical qualities:

> In fact, technical objects are not inherently beautiful in themselves, unless one is seeking a type of presentation that answers directly to aesthetic concerns; in this case there is a true distance between the technical object and the aesthetic object; it is in fact as if there were two objects, the aesthetic object enveloping and masking the technical object; this is the case for instance when one sees a water tower, build near a feudal ruin, camouflaged by added crenels and painted the same color as the old stone.

But the form of presentation of technical objects is neither the beginning nor the end of the possible beauty they have. Simondon sees beauty instead in a specific relation to the environment of the technical object that allows a correspondence and an accentuation instead of blurring:

> But in certain cases there is a beauty proper to technical objects. This beauty appears when these objects become integrated within a world, whether it be geographical or human: aesthetic feeling is then relative to this integra-tion; it is like a gesture. (196)

Simondon gives as examples electric wires that cling to the land-scape between two power poles, a car that leans into the curve, the canvas that waves in the wind, as "each technical object, mobile or fixated, can experience aesthetic epiphany by itself thus far it carries the world or fits into it" (172).

Technical objects are not beautiful by themselves but in a constel-lation that embeds them into a specific place in a landscape, or in a specific relationship with the body, or in a specific movement, or in a specific flash of signals they send. Simondon puts a lot of emphasis on this correlation: (1) the technical object is tied to a specific site (a reservoir dam, a power pole, etc.) and (2) is tied to human practice (e.g., electricity generation). Only out of this interplay emerges the aesthetic disposition of beauty. The buzzing of the power lines over a canyon whose silhouette they mimic, their glittering in the sunlight—all these appearances are much less than a surreal break with their technical functions than they are a sign of their relatedness. From this stems the experience of connectedness: from the glittering in the sunlight emerges the shining in the dark of illuminated villages and towns—connectedness creates an ensemble of imagination, knowledge, and fantasy that lets them experience something as beautiful. In this ensemble, the perceiver can see himself as inventor and not only as a user of technology and its relationship to the world within which it is embedded. The aesthetic sensations that come when walking above a big valley from where one can observe the movements of the trains, the flashing of the metal tracks, the glittering queues of cars down in the valley, find in Simondon's techno-aesthetic some grounds for why we experience them as such.

Technology and the technical object gain beauty because they "fit" into the world and because they are in the place where they are. This points back to Kant's argument about beauty, mainly that in aesthetic experience, we see ourselves as "fitting" into the world. Beauty in the sublime of contrast makes us aware of the difference, distance, and inaccessibility of nature.

Most of techno-aesthetics are looking for the sublime in technology—technology distances us from the sublime and posts it as an antagonistic second nature. An example for those aesthetic operations are the aesthetics of hardware-infused war battles, of horror and science fiction films, in which the technicity of modern warfare becomes the agent or the autonomy of the robot-like machine appears as an uncanny agent of an alien power. All leave the spectator in a state of stupor and horror of powerlessness, not to mention the new wave of dystopian films where the big machinery of surveillance gains power over the helpless subjects. Where technology is erected as natural force, even it is second to socially made nature, as technology succumbs to fetishization. The beauty of technology is by its nature a beauty of horror and overwhelming affect. It becomes fetish where its link to work, labor, and invested value is suspended.

In the attempt to look at the techno-aesthetic models of beauty as "fit" in the sense of a successful practice of establishing environmental relations in contrast to the distanciating figure of beauty as sublime, one may succeed in bridging the rupture between the two models in a dialectical figure: the redemptive aspects in the variant of "fit" become a utopian sublation of alienation, that which confronts us in the fetish as surreal artifact.

Both perspectives on beauty are tainted with some magic, once in the enchantment of a praxis that is not yet realized and on the other side in the magic promise of happiness that may be covered in the work of somebody else, who remains invisible as if by magic spell. While the fetish erects the sign of a power that has not yet appropriated the model, "fit" is a preview of possible happiness in a new practice of life yet to come.

Taking Adorno's dictum literally, that the "autonomy of art has its origin in the concealment of labor" (quoted in Benjamin 1999, 699), one can look at the aesthetic side of technology and its technical objects as the dream of the liquefaction of labor, very much in the sense that we can see in Chaplin's performance in *Modern Times* (1936) when he is first swallowed by the machine and then spit out from it as a dream walker on the sidewalks outside of the factory. Both in the beautiful appearance of the interplay between the human, nature, and technology and in the dystopian phantasmagoria, we find the idea that machines in the long run will liquidate not only the work to make machines but also the workers. Cinema, which is entirely based on this interplay between technique, technology, machines, hands, and fantasy, emanates historically exactly in the fold where the big inventions of the nineteenth century merge: electricity, the motor, transport, and media of communication. The beauty of cinema displays two sides:

a technical one as practice and one of fetishization as commodity.
Its beauty is animated by the fetish and we as spectators by the
beauty it brings afore.

Notes

1   The phrase is taken from the lovely title of Stewart Guthrie's (1993) religious-
    anthropological book *Faces in the Cloud: A New Theory of Religion.*
2   See my essay "Film as Experiment in Animation: Are Films Experiments on
    Human Beings?" (Koch 2014, 131–44).
3   The quote appears in various constellations and translations. See Wang (2016).

References

Benjamin, Walter. 1999. *The Arcades Project.* Translated by Howard Eiland and Kevin
    McLaughlin. Cambridge, Mass.: Harvard University Press.
Franco, James. 2012. "Oscar Exclusive: James Franco on Why Andy Serkis Deserves
    Credit from Actors." *Deadline Hollywood,* January 8.
Guthrie, Stewart. 1993. *Faces in the Cloud: A New Theory of Religion.* New York: Oxford
    University Press.
Koch, Gertrud. 2014. "Film as Experiment in Animation: Are Films Experiments on
    Human Beings?" In *Animating Film Theory,* edited by Karen Beckman, 131–44.
    Durham, N.C.: Duke University Press.
Marx, Karl. 1906. *Capital: A Critique of Political Economy.* Edited by Frederick Engels.
    Translated by Samuel Moore and Edward Aveling. New York: The Modern Library.
Perloff, Marjorie. 1998. "The Morphology of the Amorphous: Bill Viola's Videoscapes."
    In *Poetry on and off the Page: Essays for Emergent Occasions,* 309–21. Evanston, Ill.:
    Northwestern University Press.
Simondon, Gilbert. 2017. *On the Mode of Existence of Technical Objects.* Translated by
    Cecile Malaspina and John Rogove. Minneapolis: University of Minnesota Press.
Viola, Bill. 1995. *Reasons for Knocking at an Empty House.* Cambridge, Mass.: MIT Press.
Wang, Pan. 2016. "How TV Dating Shows Helped Change Love and Marriage in China
    Forever." *The Conversation,* June 30.
Weber, Max. 1978. *Economy and Society: An Outline of Interpretive Sociology.* Edited by
    Guehnter Roth and Claus Wittich. Berkeley: University of California Press.

For a Neganthropology of Automatic Society

Bernard Stiegler

With the advent of reticular reading and writing (Herrenschmidt 2007) via networks made accessible to everyone through the implementation, beginning in 1993, of the technologies of the World Wide Web, digital technologies have led hyperindustrial societies toward a *new stage of proletarianization*—through which the hyperindustrial age becomes the era of systemic stupidity (Stiegler 2013).

This specific age of stupidity is described by Mats Alvesson and André Spicer (2012, 1194–20) as a function of the current stage of capitalist management. Stupidity, however, as it is produced by a psychical state of stupefaction, as well as by what Adam Smith (1937, 734) called "torpor," is not just a contemporary accident imposed by the development of consumerist and speculative capitalism. It is what technological changes always produce, as they provoke what I call a doubly epokhal redoubling, where a new stage of technological development interrupts and suspends social rules and behaviors and thereby destroys social systems (in the sense of Niklas Luhmann and Bertrand Gille).

Such is also the case for digital networks. But through the latter, stupefaction and stupidity are being installed in a *new and functional way*: in such a way that disruption can *structurally and systemically short-circuit and bypass the knowledge* of psychic and collective individuals. This is what will here be called "systemic stupidity."

Remote action networks (and networks of *tele-objectivity*; Berns and Rouvroy 2013, 165) make it possible to massively delocalize production units, to form and remotely control huge markets, to structurally separate industrial capitalism and financial capitalism, and to permanently interconnect electronic financial markets, using applied mathematics to automate the "financial industry" and control these markets in real time. *Processes of automated decision-making* become functionally tied to *drive-based automatisms,* controlling consumer markets through the mediation of the mass media and, today, through the industry of traces that is the so-called data economy (that is, the economy of *personal data*).

Digital automatons have succeeded in short-circuiting the deliberative functions of the mind, and systemic stupidity, which has been installed across the board from consumers to speculators, becomes *functionally drive based,* pitting one against the other (hence this goes well beyond that "functional stupidity" described by Alvesson and Spicer 2012).

In the last few years, however, and specifically after 2008, a state of *generalized stupefaction*[1] seems to have arisen that accompanies this systemic *bêtise,* this functional stupidity.

This stupor has been caused by a *series of technological shocks* that emerged from the digital turn of 1993. The revelation of these shocks, and of their major features and consequences, has brought about a state that now verges on stunned paralysis—in particular, in the face of the hegemonic power of Google, Apple, Facebook, and Amazon (Nusca 2010), four companies that are *literally disintegrating the industrial societies* that emerged from the *Aufklärung.* The result has been what I have referred to as a feeling of "net blues," which is spreading among those who had believed or do believe in the promises of the digital era.

llllllllllllllllll

Today, the artifactual sphere that is constituted by technical individuation tends to operate as a *process of total automatization,* whose figure is the robot. The stage of total automatization is the most recent stage of the ongoing process of grammatization, that is, of the discretization and technical reproduction of human fluxes and flows—of which writing (Plato's *pharmakon*) is one stage and the machine tool is another stage (one founded on Vaucanson's automatons), and where the digital extends this to every sphere of existence, in all human societies that currently subsist—the question being to know if societies in the sense of collective individuation processes can survive such a process of automatization.

Automatism repeats. And if it is true that technical life is no longer governed by instincts but by drives, then to think automatic repetition, we must refer to Freud's discoveries in 1920, discoveries which, passing through Kierkegaard and Nietzsche, constituted the ground of Deleuze's (1994) meditation on the relationship between difference and repetition, where the automatism of repetition (or repetition as the condition of possibility of all automatism) is presented essentially as a pharmacological question (Deleuze would prefer to say "problem"), for

> if *we die of repetition we are also saved and healed by*
> *it*—healed, above all, by the other repetition. *The whole*
> *mystical game of loss and salvation* is therefore contained
> in repetition, along with the whole *theatrical game of*
> *life and death* and the whole *positive game of illness and*
> *health.* (6–7)

That what Deleuze sees as repetition is capable of producing a difference (that is, an individuation) but also a baseness (which occurs when we disindividuate), however, means that this repetition *presupposes technical exteriorization,* that is, grammatization as the *possibility of a repetition that is neither biological nor psychic, via the hypomnesic and pharmacological support* of repetition that grants a difference, that is, an individuation (and a *différance*) as well as a baseness, that is, an indifference and a disindividuation (in what

Simondon and Deleuze also describe as an "interindividuality," whereby the transindividual *loses meaning,* being no longer a *preindividual potential for individuation* but merely a formal signification through which the group *regresses* and falls into baseness).

In the nineteenth century, grammatization, which is the *technical history of the repetition of discretized mental and behavioral flows* (flows that are in this sense grammatized), which is the history of the *technical power of repetition,* leads to automation, which Marx described in the *Grundrisse,* and this constitutes a *turning point in the history of repetition*—given that today, *in industrial capitalism, economic development will occur only on the condition of putting "bad repetition" to work*—that is, by implementing the kinds of repetition *that result in baseness and indifference.*

||||||||||||||||||||

Life has had many epochs: the epoch of bacteria, of archaea, of protists and other singled-celled eukaryotes, right up to the aggregations of cells and organs that we are ourselves—ourselves, that is, these multicellular beings who cannot do without nonliving organs, artifacts, prostheses, and, eventually, today, automata. As I prepared for this conference, for example, I searched among the masses of tertiary retentions, which are mnemotechnical traces, and which we (living technicians) have produced for two million years (and organized in the form of knowledge), in order to find out about archaea, using Google and then Wikipedia, the latter being a collaboratively produced site, although what is usually forgotten is that it is also highly reliant on so-called bots, which is an abbreviation for robots, when, by the latter, we mean logical and algorithmic automatons that are "mainly used to perform repetitive tasks that automation allows to be performed at high speed."

The *differentiation of the living* unfolds from the parthenogenesis of single-celled organisms right up to the higher vertebrates like ourselves, endowed with both an endoskeleton *and* an exoskeleton and surrounded by the exo-organisms and organizations that are human societies producing a collective individuation founded on artificial organs, and passing along the way through the sexuation of multicellular bodies lacking a nervous system, such as plants, through invertebrate animals protected by an exoskeleton, such as the snail, the crab, the insect, and so on. *Today,* long after technical organs first appeared, this differentiation of the living has led to the *automatic differentiation of the nonliving,* the production of organs and organizations where the difference between organic and inorganic becomes blurred in becoming industrial—at the cost of an indifferentiation of life (that is, its decline), a loss of biodiversity as much as of "cultural diversity."

At each step of this history of the *struggle of negentropy against the entropy that results from its becoming technical*—and it is perhaps precisely this that defines the "pharmacological," in other words, to have, in a Janus-like way, one face that is negentropic and another that is entropic—*each epoch of life implements new conditions of automatic repetition in which differences are produced,* differences that we generally relate to forms of autonomy, of the *psukhē* defined by Aristotle as having three types, and as self-movement in autopoiesis in the theory of enaction, and passing through thinking as dialogue with oneself according to Plato, or the conquest of majority [*Mündigkeit*] in the Kantian sense (Kant 1991, 54–60).

But to understand what we are, and to which we will have been under way for at least two million years, or four million, if we believe Leroi-Gourhan, and to understand it *correctly,* all this must be thought with the concepts of mineral, vital, and psychosocial individuation.

Psychosocial individuation is the *second epoch of automatism* (there is no mineral automatism, and this is why Canguilhem can claim that there are no mineral monsters: when life reproduces itself, it repeats life in an automatic way, but within vital reproduction, there can be deviations that we can call monstrous insofar as they do not automatically repeat the schema of the organic form that is reproducing itself—and this is what cannot happen to a crystal).

The advent of psychosocial individuation, however, will in turn eventually lead to a generalized industrial automatization founded on automation such as it began in the nineteenth century with that fact described by Andrew Ure (and cited by Marx 1973, 690–712[2]) as a "vast automaton."

A *new epoch of psychic and collective individuation* thus emerges, which would take us into a process that would perhaps not be posthuman—because humanism, as the question of knowing what humanity is, is not a true question, if it is true that man is the one who individuates himself with technics such that he constantly *becomes other* and such that the human adopts the inhuman or *becomes inhuman as a result of failing to reach the point of human-ness* and from *failing to adapt himself by individuating himself,* that is, from a failure to think and to realize this thought concretely—but rather an *inversion of exteriorization, where it becomes interiorization* such that this technical internalization seems to induce a psychic disinteriorization.

There is no exteriorization without interiorization—except in the case of proletarianization, the precise goal of which is to submit the proletarianized to an exteriorization of its knowledge without the need for reinternalizing what has been exteriorized. Today the evidence of neuroscience opens new vistas in relation to these questions. When we see how neuroeconomics "applies" this evidence, we can better grasp how significant are the stakes of what I believe we should describe as the age of generalized automatization.

ııııııııııııııı

The hyperindustrial societies that have grown out of the ruins of the industrial democracies constitute the third stage of completed proletarianization: after the loss of work-knowledge [*savoir-faire*] in the nineteenth century, then of life-knowledge [*savoir-vivre*] in the twentieth, there arises in the twenty-first century the age of the loss of theoretical knowledge—as if the cause of our being stunned was an *absolutely unthinkable* becoming.

With the *total automatization* made possible by digital technology, theories, those most sublime fruits of idealization and identification, are deemed obsolete—and along with them, scientific method itself. So at least we are told by Chris Anderson (2008) in "The End of Theory: The Data Deluge Makes the Scientific Method Obsolete."[3]

Founded on the *self-production* of digital traces, and dominated by automatisms that exploit these traces, hyperindustrial societies are undergoing the proletarianization of theoretical knowledge, just as broadcasting analog traces via television resulted in the proletarianization of life-knowledge, and just as the submission of the body of the laborer to mechanical traces inscribed in machines resulted in the proletarianization of work-knowledge.

Just like written traces, in which Socrates already saw the risk of proletarianization contained in any exteriorization of knowledge (Stiegler 2010)—the apparent paradox being that *knowledge can be constituted only through its exteriorization*—digital, analog, and mechanical traces are what I call tertiary retentions.

Writing (whether ideographic, alphabetic, or digital) is a kind of tertiary retention. The brain is the site of secondary retentions, which are, in Husserl's (1991) sense, memories of those perceptions that are woven together from what Husserl called "primary retentions."

Retention refers to what is retained, through a mnesic function itself constituent of a consciousness, that is, of a psychic apparatus. Within this psychic retention, a secondary retention, which is the constitutive element of a mental state that is always based on memory, was originally a *primary* retention: by "primary" is meant that which is retained in the course of a *perception,* and through the *process* of this perception, but *in the present,* which means that primary retention is *not yet a memory,* even if it is *already* a retention. A primary retention is what, in the course of a present experience, is destined to become a secondary retention of somebody who has lived this experience that has become past—secondary because, no longer being perceived, it is imprinted in the memory of the one who had the experience, and from which it may be reactivated.

But a retention, as the result of a flux and emerging from the temporal course of experience, may also become *tertiary,* through the spatialization in which consists the grammatization (and more generally, in which consists *any technical materialization process*) of the flow of retentions. This mental reality can thus be *projected onto a support that is neither cerebral nor psychic but rather technical.*

When Gilles Deleuze referred to what he called "control societies," he was already heralding the arrival of the hyperindustrial age. The destructive capture of attention and desire is what occurs in and through those control societies described by Deleuze in terms of the noncoercive modulation exercised by television on consumers at the end of the twentieth century. These societies of control appear at the end of the consumerist epoch, and their effect is to make way for the transition to the hyperindustrial epoch.

In the automatic society that Deleuze was never to know, but which with Félix Guattari he anticipated (in particular, when they referred to *dividuals*; Deleuze 1995, 180), control passes through the mechanical liquidation of discernment, or in Greek, *to krinon*—from *krinein,* a verb that has the same root as *krisis,* "decision." The discernment that Kant called "understanding" [*Verstand*] has been automatized as the *analytical* power delegated to algorithms and executed through sensors and actuators but outside of any intuition in the Kantian sense, that is, outside any experience (this being the situation that occupies the attention of Anderson 2008).

|||||||||||||||||||

Almost a decade after the collapse of 2008, it is still not clear how best to characterize this *event*: as *crisis, mutation, metamorphosis*? All these terms are *metaphors*—they are not yet thinking. *Krisis,* which has a long history—in Hippocrates, it refers to a decisive turning point in the course of an illness—is also the origin of all critique, of all decision exercised by *to krinon* as the power to judge on the basis of criteria. *Mutation* is understood today primarily in relation to biology—even if, in French, to be *muté* generally refers in everyday life to being transferred to another posting. And *metamorphosis* is a zoological term that comes from the Greek, by way of Ovid.

Approaching ten years since this event occurred, it seems that the *proletarianization of minds* and, more precisely, the *proletarianiza-tion of the noetic faculties of theorization,* and, in this sense, of *scien-tific, moral, aesthetic, and political deliberation*—combined with the proletarianization of sensibility and affect in the twentieth century, and with the proletarianization of the gestures of the worker in the nineteenth century—is both the *trigger for* and the *result of* this continuing "crisis." As a result, no decisions are taken, and we fail to arrive at any turning point, any "bifurcation" (in Deleuze's terms). In the meantime, all of the toxic aspects that lie at the origins of this crisis continue to be consolidated.

When a triggering factor is also an outcome, we find ourselves within a spiral. This spiral can be very fruitful and worthwhile, or it can enclose us—*absent new criteria*—in a vicious circle that we can then describe as a "downward spiral" that takes us from bad to worse.

I believe with Francis Jutand (2013, 9) that the *postlarval state* in which the 2008 crisis has been left implies that we should refer to it in terms of metamorphosis rather than mutation: what is going on here is not biological, even if biology comes into play via biotech-nology, and, in certain respects, in an almost proletarianized way.[4] Human evolution is the result of an exosomatic organogenesis, as was shown by Alfred J. Lotka (1956) and Nicholas Georgescu-Rœgen (1971). In the exosomatic form of life, what drives evolution (that is, organogenesis) is not biology but economics—as a process of artificial selection for which knowledge is the driver and the provider of the criteria of selection.

With the advent of the Industrial Revolution, which is also to say of the Anthropocene, exosomatization entered a stage in which knowledge was replaced by automation—beginning with the skills of manual workers. In today's automated society, all forms of knowledge are being short-circuited by systems of digital tertiary retention operating four million times more quickly than the nervous system of the human noetic body.

Claiming that this is a metamorphosis—which can also be called "disruptive innovation"—does not mean that there is no *krisis* or that we need not take account of the critical labor for which it calls. It means that *this critical labor is precisely what this metamorphosis seems to render impossible,* thanks precisely to the fact that it consists *above all* in the proletarianization of theoretical knowledge, which is critical knowledge, in a world where today the digital reaches speeds of two hundred thousand kilometers per second, or two-thirds the speed of light, which is some four million times faster than the speed of nerve impulses. It is for this reason that I propose understanding the enduring nature of this crisis on the basis of the metaphor of the chrysalis, where it becomes a matter of how to transform the toxicity of the new exosomatic organs into new forms of knowledge.

The *stupefying situation* in which the current experience of automatic society consists establishes a new mental context (stupefaction) within which systemic stupidity undoubtedly proliferates (as functional stupidity, drive-based capitalism, and industrial populism), but where this also reflects the rise of a *new concern*—which, *if it is not turned into panic,* and instead becomes a fertile *skepsis,* could prove to be the *beginning of a new understanding of the situation*— and the genesis of new criteria, or categories: this amounts to the question of what I call *categorial invention.*

Digital technology—which, according to Clarence Herrenschmidt, establishes the age of *reticular writing*—is based on the computer, which, more than anything, is an artificial organ of *automated categorization,* that is, it automatically produces digital tertiary retentions on the basis of other digital tertiary retentions. The automation of categorization makes it possible for *operations of analysis and understanding to be delegated to digital systems.*

Interpretation cannot be delegated to an analytical system of tertiary retentions: on the contrary, it always consists in *deciding between possibilities opened up by tertiary retentions,* but *these tertiary retentions are not themselves capable of choosing between,* however automated they may be—for here, *to choose means, precisely, to disautomatize,* that is, to create what Gilles Deleuze called a *bifurcation.*

In Kant, the difference between *analysis and synthesis* grounds the difference between *understanding and reason.* I have argued that analytical understanding is made possible by tertiary retentions insofar as they belong to a process of grammatization (such as the analysis of a written poem, an analysis made possible by writing), grammatization being the discretization, reproduction, and spatialization of temporal flows.

But *synthesis too* is made possible by analytic tertiary retentions: they *affect* the noetic psychic individual because, spatialized, they trace and make public potential conflicts of interpretation—pharmacological conflicts between peers that affect these noetic individuals. And these affects, the critical convergence of which is called *reason,* are *what trigger interpretations.* It is from this perspective that we should read Spinoza.

Through the process of transindividuation, the arbitration of these conflicts is "certified." *Certification processes may themselves be either analytic or synthetic*—and in this case, they are elaborated on the basis of interpretations that result in *categorial inventions. Hermeneia* is in fact that which, through glosses and commentaries of all kinds, invents and generates new categories (whether analytic or synthetic) through which knowledge is transformed. New categories are certified when they are recognized by peers via analytic certifications that may on occasion be automated—whereas synthetic certifications, which result in categorial inventions that provoke bifurcations, can *never* be delegated to systems, precisely because they are processes of interpretation.

This new understanding or intelligence would be that which, inverting the toxic logic of the *pharmakon,* would give rise to a *new hyperindustrial age that would constitute an automatic society founded on deproletarianization* [5]—and which would provide an exit from the chrysalis of *noetic hymenoptera*[6]—that is, to a society based on the valorization of positive externalities and capacities (in Sen's sense): on a contributive economy of pollination (Stiegler 2016).

ııııııııııııııııı

The proletarianization of the gestures of work amounts to the proletarianization of the conditions of the worker's *subsistence.*

The proletarianization of sensibility, of sensory life, and the proletarianization of social relations, all of which are replaced by conditioning, amounts to the proletarianization of the conditions of the citizen's *existence.*

The proletarianization of minds or spirits, that is, of the noetic faculties enabling theorization and deliberation, is the proletarianization of the conditions of scientific *consistence* (including the human and social sciences).

In the hyperindustrial stage, *hypercontrol* is established through a process of generalized automatization. This represents a step beyond the control-through-modulation discovered and analyzed by Deleuze (1995): now, the noetic faculties of theorization and deliberation are short-circuited by the *current operator of proletarianization,* which is *digital tertiary retention*—just as analog tertiary retention was in the twentieth century the operator of the proletarianization of life-knowledge, and just as mechanical tertiary retention was in the nineteenth century the operator of the proletarianization of work-knowledge.

By *artificially retaining something through the material and spatial copying of a mnesic and temporal element,* tertiary retention modifies the relations between the psychic retentions of *perception* that Husserl (1991) referred to as *primary* retentions and the psychic retentions of *memory* that he called *secondary* retentions.

Over time, tertiary retention evolves, and this leads to modifications of the *play* between primary retentions and secondary retentions, resulting in *processes of transindividuation* that are each time specific, that is, specific epochs of what Simondon called the *transindividual.*

In the course of processes of transindividuation, founded on successive epochs of tertiary retention, meanings form that are shared by psychic individuals, thereby constituting collective individuals themselves forming "societies." Shared by psychic individuals within collective individuals of all kinds, the meanings formed during transindividuation processes constitute the transindividual as an ensemble of collective secondary retentions within which collective protentions are formed—which are the *expectations* typical of an epoch.

If, according to the Anderson article to which we previously referred, so-called Big Data heralds the "end of theory" (Anderson 2008)—Big Data technology designating what is also called "high-performance computing" carried out on massive data sets, whereby the treatment of data in the form of digital tertiary retentions occurs *in real time* (at the speed of light) and on a *global scale* and at the level of billions of gigabytes of data, operating through data-capture systems that are located everywhere around the planet and in almost every relational system that a society constitutes—it is because digital tertiary retention and the algorithms that allow it to be both produced and exploited thereby also make it possible for *reason as a synthetic faculty to be short-circuited* thanks to the *extremely high speeds* at which this automated analytical faculty of *understanding* is capable of operating (Stiegler 2016).

‖‖‖‖‖‖‖‖‖‖‖‖‖

In automatic society, those digital networks referred to as "social" networks channel such expressions by submitting them to mandatory protocols, to which psychic individuals bend because they are drawn to do so by the so-called *network effect,* which, with the addition of social networking, becomes an *automated herd effect,* that is, a highly mimetic situation. It therefore amounts to a new form of *artificial crowd* in the sense Freud (1955, 124) gave to this expression.[7]

Ten years ago, I compared TV and radio programs and channels to the constitution of artificial and conventional crowds such as they were analyzed by Freud—for which he gives the examples of army and church.

The constitution of groups or crowds and the conditions under which they can pass into action were subjects analyzed by Gustave Le Bon, cited at length by Freud:

> The most striking peculiarity presented by a psychological crowd [*Masse*] is the following. Whoever be the individuals that compose it, however like or unlike be their mode of life, their occupations, their character, or their intelligence, the fact that they have been transformed into a crowd puts them in possession of a sort of collective mind which makes them feel, think, and act in a manner quite different from that in which each individual of them would feel, think, and act were he in a state of isolation. There are certain ideas and feelings which do not come into being, or do not transform themselves into acts except in the case of individuals forming a crowd.
>
> The psychological group is a provisional being formed of heterogeneous elements, which for a moment are combined, exactly as the cells which constitute a living body form by their reunion a new being which displays characteristics very different from those possessed by each of the cells singly. (Freud, quoted in Le Bon 1895, 72–73)[8]

On the basis of Le Bon's analyses, Freud showed that there are also "artificial" and "conventional" crowds, which he analyzes through the examples of the church and the army.

The program industries, too, however, also form, every single day, and specifically through the mass broadcast of programs, such "artificial crowds." The latter become, as masses (and Freud refers precisely to *Massenpsychologie*), the permanent, everyday mode of life in the industrial democracies, which are at the same time what I call industrial tele-cracies—wherein the process of identification with the leader becomes identification with movie stars and TV presenters.

Generated by digital tertiary retention, *connected* artificial crowds constitute the economy of "crowdsourcing," which should be understood in multiple senses—one dimension of which would be the so-called cognitariat (Newfield 2010). To a large degree, Big Data is utilized by technologies that exploit the potential of crowdsourcing in its many forms, engineered by social networking and data science.

Through the network effect, through the artificial crowds that create (more than a billion psychic individuals on Facebook), and through the crowdsourcing that it can exploit through Big Data, it is possible

- *to generate the production and autocapture* by individuals of those tertiary retentions that are "personal data," spatializing their psychosocial temporalities;
- *to intervene in the processes of transindividuation* that are woven between them by utilizing these "personal data" at the speed of light via circuits that are formed automatically and *performatively*;
- through these circuits, and through the collective secondary retentions that they form automatically, and no longer transindividually, *to intervene in return, almost immediately, on psychic secondary retentions,* which is also to say, on protentions, expectations, and, ultimately, personal behavior: it thus becomes possible to *remotely control, one by one,* the members of a network—this is so-called personalization.

The internet is a *pharmakon* that can thus become a technique for hypercontrol and social dis-integration. Without a new politics of individuation, that is, without a formation of attention geared toward the specific tertiary retentions that make possible the new technical milieu, it will inevitably become an agent of dissociation.

〰〰〰〰〰〰

The pharmacological character of the digital age has become more or less clear to those who belong to it, resulting in what I am calling "net blues": the state of fact constituted by this new age of tertiary retention *has failed to provide a new state of law. On the contrary,* it has liquidated the rule of law as produced by the retentional systems of the bygone epoch. Property law, for example, has been directly challenged by activists through their practices in relation to free software, and through reflecting on the "commons," including some young artists who are attempting to devise a new economic and political framework for their thinking.

These questions must, however, be seen as elements of an *epistemic* and *epistemological* transition from fact to law, a transition effected by referring canonically to apodictic experience—projecting law beyond fact. The passage from fact to law is first a matter of discovering *in facts* the *necessity of interpreting them,* that is, of projecting *beyond the facts* themselves, but also *on the basis of facts* that are not themselves self-sufficient—projecting them onto another plane toward which they beckon: that of a consistence through which and in which we must "believe."

This other plane is that of negentropy. If we are now living in the Anthropocene, this state of fact is not sustainable: we must pass to a state of law in which negentropy becomes the criteria of every type of value, the value of value, and this is why we must enter into the Neganthropocene. This requires a neganthropology, that is, an economy of the *pharmakon* that is produced by the process of exosomatization, where the exosomatic organs are always both entropic and negentropic and where no biological law prescribes their arrangements.

In such a neganthropological situation, belief means the ability to project possibilities for bifurcation, in a system that is on the way to becoming closed and requires a change that by itself the system cannot calculate. Such possibilities are those prescribed and certified by work-knowledge, life-knowledge, and conceptual knowledge, that is, by knowledge of how to live, do, and think.

Automatization is bringing with it a massive macroeconomic problem: the decline in purchasing power that results from rising unemployment. This situation requires new criteria for the redistribution of productivity gains. And we believe—at Ars Industrialis, and at the Institut de recherche et d'innovation, as we together develop a ten-year experiment with a region in the north of Paris, Plaine Commune[9]—that a genuinely contributory economy must be an economy of neganthropy based on a contributory income. This must be a conditional income that allows individuals to be paid to increase their capabilities, on the condition that they contribute to any kind of "neganthropic" enterprise, as has been the case in France for those working in the performing arts and the cinema.

This is so because in France, there is a scheme that indemnifies against unemployment those workers known as *intermittents du spectacle.* This scheme should become a model for a *law of work* in an economy of contribution, just as we believe that free software, *inasmuch as it is a challenge to the industrial division of labor,* should constitute a model for the *organization of work.* The widespread generalization of this organization of work requires a *contributory organology* that remains entirely to be developed[10]—in the first place, with the free software communities that have been around now for thirty years.

The scheme covering these occasional workers is even older: it was established in 1936 and has since been much transformed. It was threatened for the first time in 2003 and became the object of a struggle, in relation to which Antonella Corsani and Maurizio Lazzarato wrote in 2008,

> It is in reality a struggle whose stakes are the employment of time. To the injunction to increase the time of employment, that is, the proportion of life occupied by

employment, the experience of intermittence opposes the
multiplicity of the times of employment. (121)

In other words, the intermittence scheme completely rearranges
employment and time, precisely by considering the *work of the
"intermittent" as time outside employment*—as *capacitation* and
individuation and hence as much more than just earnings and
production. Corsani and Lazzarato therefore conclude that we
must "interrogate the very category of 'work'":

> If there is activity during periods of unemployment, but
> also during the time of so-called living, during the time
> called free, during the time of training, until it flows over
> into the time for rest, what then does work encompass,
> given that it contains a multiplicity of activities and het-
> erogeneous temporalities? (121)

Amartya Sen (2000, xii) relates "capacitation" and "capability" to
the development of freedom, which is to say, in the first place,
free time, which he defines as always being both individual and
collective:

> We have to see individual freedom as a social
> commitment.

In this way, Sen remains faithful to both Kantian and Socratic perspectives. Capability constitutes the basis of economic dynamism
and development, and it does so as freedom:

> Expansion of freedom is viewed, in this approach,
> both as the primary end and as the principal means of
> development. (36)

Freedom, in Sen's definition, is therefore a form of agency: the
power to act.

Sen's comparative example of the incapacitating effects of consum-
erism (that is, in his terms, of the indicators of affluence) is well
known: the black residents of Harlem have a lower life expectancy

than the people of Bangladesh, and this is precisely a question of their "agency."

Freedom is here a question of knowledge insofar as it is a capability that is always both individual and collective—and this means individuated both psychically and collectively. It was on this basis that Sen devised the Human Development Index to form a contrast with the Economic Growth Index.

I would like to extend Sen's propositions by means of a different analysis, one that leads to other questions. In particular, consideration must be given to the question of what relations psychic and collective individuals can forge with automatons, in order to achieve individual and collective bifurcations within an industrial and economic system that, having become massively automatized, tends also to become closed.

The Anthropocene, insofar as it is an "Entropocene," amounts to accomplished nihilism: it produces an unsustainable leveling of all values that requires a leap into a "transvaluation" capable of giving rise to a "general economy" in Georges Bataille's (1988) sense, whose work I have elsewhere tried to show involves a reconsideration of libidinal economy. The movement I am describing here is no doubt not a transvaluation in a strict Nietzschean sense. Rather, it is an invitation to reread Nietzsche with respect to questions of disorder and order, that is, also, entropy and negentropy, that in the following will be understood in terms of becoming and future.

⠀⠀⠀⠀⠀⠀⠀⠀⠀⠀⠀⠀ꞮꞮꞮꞮꞮꞮꞮꞮꞮꞮꞮꞮꞮꞮꞮꞮꞮꞮꞮ

If there is to be a future, and not just a becoming, the value of tomorrow will lie in the constitutive negentropy of the economy-to-come of the Neganthropocene. For such an economy, the practical and functional differentiation between becoming and future must form its criteria of evaluation—only in so doing will it be possible to overcome the systemic entropy in which the Anthropocene consists. This economy requires a shift from anthropology to neganthropology, where the latter is founded on what I call general organology and on a pharmacology: the *pharmakon,* that is, technics in general as both poison and remedy, is the artifact and as such the condition of hominization, that is, an organogenesis of artifactual organs and organizations, but it always produces both entropy and negentropy, and hence it is always also a threat to hominization.

The problem raised by such a perspective on the future is to know how to *evaluate* or *measure* negentropy. Referred to as negative entropy by Erwin Schrödinger and as anti-entropy by Francis Bailly and Giuseppe Longo, negentropy is always defined in relation to an observer (see the work of Atlan 1979; Morin 1992)—that is, it is always described in relation to a *locality in time as well as in space that it, as such, produces,* and that it *differentiates* within a more or less homogeneous space (and this is why a neganthropology is always also a geography). What appears entropic from one angle is negentropic from another angle.

Knowledge, as work-knowledge (that is, knowledge of what to do so that *I do not myself collapse* and am not led into chaos), as life-knowledge (that is, knowledge that *enriches and individuates the social organization in which I live without destroying it*), and as conceptual knowledge (that is, *knowledge the inheritance of which occurs only by passing through its transformation, and which is transformed only by being reactivated* through a process of what Socrates called *anamnesis* [Plato 1961], a process that, in the West, structurally exceeds its locality)—knowledge, in all these forms, is *always a way of collectively defining what is negentropic in this or that field of human existence.*

What we call the *inhuman* is a denial of the negentropic possibilities of the human, that is, a denial of its noetic freedom and, as a result, its *agency.* What Sen describes as freedom and capability must be conceived from this cosmic perspective and related to Alfred Whitehead's "speculative cosmology" as constituting a negentropic potentiality—as the potential for *openness* of a *localized* system that, for that being we refer to as "human," may always once again become closed. Or, in Whitehead's (1929, 18–19) terms, human beings may always relapse, decay into simpler forms, that is, become inhuman.

Today, in the Anthropocene, which with total automation is reaching a threshold of disruptiveness, the *context* of the task of thinking conceived as therapeutics is one in which automatisms of all kinds are being technologically integrated by digital automatisms. The unique and very specific aspect of this situation is the way that digital tertiary retention succeeds in totally rearranging the assemblages or montages of psychic and collective retentions and protentions. The challenge is to invert this situation by having an *ars* of hypercontrol instead reach toward a new idea of work as disautomatization, which would arise out of today's dis-integrating automatization.

Translated by Daniel Ross

Notes

1 Stupefaction, which is not merely stupidity, but which is in general its cause, is the typical modality of our age, insofar as it is the age of disruptive innovation in the epoch of what, already in 1996, I referred to as *disorientation* (Stiegler 2009).

2 This is the so-called Fragment on Machines.

3 I argued in *What Makes Life Worth Living* (Stiegler 2013) that Alan Greenspan's defense when confronted with the failure of the financial system was already based on the argument that in an automated financial economy, it is no longer possible to theorize, and that from this, it followed that he had no responsibility to act after the series of economic catastrophes that were caused by the dogmas that he applied during the subprime era, from making Madoff chairman of NASDAQ to the decision not to rescue Lehman Brothers.

4 On this topic, see Stiegler (2013, chapter 7).

5 This refers to the possibility of deproletarianization through the socialization of factors that produce proletarianization and is the hypothesis that governs the new critique of political economy advocated by Ars Industrialis.

6 See the French Wikipedia entry on "hymenoptera": "The order hymenoptera includes herbivores, pollinators, and a wide range of entomophagous insects that play a central role in maintaining natural equilibrium. The entomophagous insects comprise the majority of parasitoids (43% of hymenoptera species that have been described) but also predators. The actual number of hymenoptera is estimated at somewhere between one and three million species, divided

into a hundred families. Many species have not yet been described, or even discovered."

7   Translation modified.

8   Translation modified.

9   See http://recherchecontributive.org/.

10   This will be the theme of the final chapter of Bernard Stiegler, *Automatic Society, Volume 2: The Future of Knowledge.* Concerning concepts derived from computer science, see Hui (2016).

References

Alvesson, Mats, and André Spicer. 2012. "A Stupidity-Based Theory of Organizations." *Journal of Management Studies* 49: 1194–220.

Anderson, Chris. 2008. "The End of Theory: The Data Deluge Makes the Scientific Method Obsolete." *Wired,* June 23.

Atlan, Henri. 1979. *Entre le cristal et la fumée.* Paris: Le Seuil.

Bataille, Georges. 1988. *The Accursed Share: Vol. 1. Consumption.* New York: Zone.

Berns, Thomas, and Antoinette Rouvroy. 2013. "Gouvernementalité algorithmique et perspectives d'émancipation." *Réseaux* 1 (177): 163–96.

Corsani, Antonella, and Maurizio Lazzarato. 2008. *Intermittents et précaires.* Paris: Amsterdam.

Deleuze, Gilles. 1994. *Difference and Repetition.* London: Athlone.

Deleuze, Gilles. 1995. "Postscript on Control Societies." In *Negotiations,* 177–82. New York: Columbia University Press.

Freud, Sigmund. 1955. "Group Psychology and the Analysis of the Ego." *Standard Edition* 18: 65–144.

Georgescu-Rœgen, Nicholas. 1971. *The Entropy Law and the Economic Process.* Cambridge, Mass.: Harvard University Press.

Herrenschmidt, Clarisse. 2007. *Les Trois Écritures: Langue, nombre, code.* Paris: Gallimard.

Hui, Yuk. 2016. *On the Existence of Digital Objects.* Minneapolis: University of Minnesota Press.

Husserl, Edmund. 1991. *On the Phenomenology of the Consciousness of Internal Time.* Dordrecht, Netherlands: Kluwer.

Jutland, Francis. 2013. *La Métamorphose numérique: Vers une société de la connaisance et de la cooperation.* Paris: Alternatives.

Kant, Immanuel. 1991. "An Answer to the Question: 'What Is Enlightenment?'" In *Political Writings,* 54–60. Cambridge: Cambridge University Press.

Le Bon, Gustave. 1895. *Psychologie des foules.* Paris: Félix Alcan.

Lotka, Alfred J. 1956. *Elements of Mathematical Biology.* New York: Dover.

Marx, Karl. 1973. *Grundrisse: Foundations of the Critique of Political Economy (Rough Draft).* London: Penguin.

Morin, Edgar. 1992. *The Nature of Nature.* New York: Peter Lang.

Newfield, Christopher. 2010. "The Structure and Silence of the Cognitariat." *Eurozine,* February 5.

Nusca, Andrew. 2010. "Kleiner Perkins' Doerr: Google, Facebook, Amazon, Apple the **47**
'Four Great Horsemen of the Internet.'" *ZDNet,* May 24.

Plato. 1961. *Meno.* Edited by R. S. Bluck. Cambridge: Cambridge University Press.

Sen, Amartya. 2000. *Development as Freedom.* New York: Alfred A. Knopf.

Smith, Adam. 1937. *An Inquiry into the Nature and Causes of the Wealth of Nations.* New
York: Modern Library.

Stiegler, Bernard. 2009. *Technics and Time 2: Disorientation.* Stanford, Calif.: Stanford
University Press.

Stiegler, Bernard. 2010. *For a New Critique of Political Economy.* Cambridge: Polity.

Stiegler, Bernard. 2013. *What Makes Life Worth Living: On Pharmacology.* Cambridge:
Polity.

Stiegler, Bernard. 2016. *Automatic Society: Vol. 1. The Future of Work.* Cambridge:
Polity.

Whitehead, Alfred North. 1929. *The Function of Reason.* Princeton, N.J.: Princeton
University Press.

The Ecosystem Is an Apparatus: From Machinic Ecology to the Politics of Resilience

Thomas Pringle

More than ever today, nature has become inseparable from culture; and if we are to understand the interactions between ecosystems, the mechanosphere, and the social and individual universes of reference, we have to learn to think "transversally." As the waters of Venice are invaded by monstrous, mutant algae, so our television screens are peopled and saturated by "degenerate" images and utterances. In the realm of social ecology, Donald Trump and his ilk—another form of algae—are permitted to proliferate unchecked. In the name of renovation, Trump takes over whole districts of New York or Atlantic City, raises rents, and squeezes out tens of thousands of poor families. Those who Trump condemns to homelessness are the social equivalent of the dead fish of environmental ecology.

—Félix Guattari, *The Three Ecologies*

Animate | Automate: Machine Components for Current Technopolitical Thought

Animate derives from the Latin *animatus,* in the sense of "giving life to." *Automate,* from *automation,* originates in the Greek *automatos,* the "acting of itself." For Gertrud Koch and Bernard Stiegler, these terms of media provide a lens through which to conceive machines as philosophical configurations of culture, technology, aesthetics, and labor.

Both *animate* and *automate* illustrate how "Machine" works as a theoretical concept and help differentiate "Machine" as a term of media from "Technology." *Machine,* from the Greek *Mākhaná,* denotes a tool, and derivations variously indicate means or strategies (machinations), abilities, instruments of power, or tricks. While technology implements scientific knowledge, machines are specifically tied to labor, work, and power. Animation, from one perspective, concerns the ontology of the machine and the manner by which machines bring matter to life. More precisely, animation describes the machine in its capacity to set matter into movement, whether through mechanism or illusion. Automation, from another perspective, focuses on the machine's technical procedure, repetition, and dispersal in time. Machines change automatically, whether through formal differentiation, deterioration, reproduction, or self-replication. While these terms are distinct characterizations of the functionality of machines, the animation of life and the repetitive automation of production are not entirely distinct, as illustrated by Stiegler (2015, 16) in a recent interview, in which he explains that the operative properties of machines and life are functionally analogous: "Life is automatic. A Biological cell, for example, is a sequence of instructions and this sequence of instructions is automatic. The reproduction of life is automatic. . . . So automatic repetition is really the basis of life." What is the work of animate and automate as each term purports to describe in *technical* terms the operation of an inhuman process, be it organic or technological? What supports the analogous description of organic and technical development? Given the proximity of the animating and automating functions of the machine—whether that is illusion, labor, work, production, reproduction, or self-replication—the machine's privileged status as a site of conceptual translation between those vital mechanisms that bring-to-life, and the mechanical codes that drive repetition, mark this volume's field of theoretical inquiry.

Between animate and automate, the concept of the machine
answers questions about contemporary media technologies
that operate across both great and microscopic scales. When
perceived from within a digital paradigm that understands people,
nature, and infrastructure in the calculable rubric of information,
the magnitude of machines and their mass dispersal becomes
a political problem. We get close to machines. Through use, we
develop intimate, habitual, and embodied relations with complex
machinery and take in the knowledge of the world that they relay.
Machines have grown to span continents, like electrical grids,
but the digital turn arguably extends the purview of machines
to the scale of smart cities, undersea cable networks, or satellite
communication systems. Then, we debate the consequences of the
embodied sensibilities opened by the knowledge–infrastructure
couplings inherent to encounters with machines too large or familiar to see, much less operate on our own. Machines, by magnitude,
complexity, availability, or mass production, are inherently social
devices. They never leave us alone.

Koch, in "Animation of the Technical and the Quest for Beauty"
(chapter 1 of this volume), frames and reframes the human body,
and the machine's animation of the human's perceptive faculties,
against a technoecological drama. Situating the labor, beauty, and
practicality of machines within broader patterns of social organization guiding the human use of technology, "machines" become
"agents in a field of techniques." Her theory departs from tradi-
tions of media ecology initiated by Marshall McLuhan—wherein
technological mediums are extensions of the body's form—by
sharpening the function of illusion and fetish in the animating purpose of the machine. This move accords to a "paradigm change:
[when] machines are no longer extensions of organs" but "media
that performatively intervene in our action." Alternatively, Stiegler
prepares readers "For a Neganthropology of Automatic Society"
(chapter 2 of this volume) by raising automation as a concept
illustrating the repetitive production of proletarian knowledge
that he distills as the characteristic of work in digital network

culture. Referencing Chris Anderson's proclamation that Big Data's processes of automatic calculation render the scientific method obsolete, Stiegler cautions that the production of theoretical knowledge itself is lost to the automation of human thought as it is reticulated within the speed and form of automated machines and their retentive functionality for autonomous computation. Hence, "in today's automated society, all forms of knowledge are being short-circuited by systems of digital tertiary retention operating four million times more quickly than the nervous system of the human noetic body." Koch and Stiegler locate the machine—in its animating and automating capacities—as a primary object for critique in a social environment that is as much technological as it is natural.

With these two functions of the machine in mind—the animation of life and the automation of production—I see the ecosystem as a term of media that helps articulate the machine's particular concep-tual value. The ecosystem is a variety of machine that, like *animate* and *automate,* easily slips between operative functions found in both the technical and the organic. As a hybrid term melding the study of the environmental–organic flows of biophysical reality (ecology) and the mechanisms of networked cohesion (system), eco-system offers a way to theorize how machines mimic the animate and productive forces of life, while accounting for the automatic conversion of natural resources into energy, commodities, and waste through repetition and self-regulation. Ecosystem, as I outline later, is a unique term of media that holds a strategically valuable historical relationship to proximate concepts, including economy, the psyche, apparatus, and digital information. Exploring these relationships provides a way to synthesize the animate qualities of life's cascade—ecology—with the automated patterns of production both defining energy flow in nature and giving the capacity for modes of work in the economy. The ecosystem, I argue, is also a term of media, advantageously positioned as a machine that maps the recursive traffic between animate and automate, ecological and economic systems.

What does analyzing text, or media, as a part of an "ecology" actually mean?[1] Does enlisting the term *ecology* for critical inquiry easily assume an immanent relationship between systems of discourse and the field of nondiscursive actions that constitute the interactivity of both technological and biophysical reality? How does the history of the science of ecology—the study of the flow of natural systems—influence the reception of the ecosystem as the term becomes a critical method in the humanities?

The epistemology outlined by cyberneticist Gregory Bateson (1972) in *Steps to an Ecology of Mind* is exemplary of an ecological methodology, with one of the book's direct influences in social and political theory being Gilles Deleuze and Félix Guattari's ([1980] 1987) *A Thousand Plateaus: Capitalism and Schizophrenia.* The marriage of Bateson's concepts with an explicit environmental political program is expressed most clearly in Guattari's (1989) later work *The Three Ecologies.* Guattari's thesis, quoted in the epigraph, forwards an imperative to think *transversally across* the delineated bounds of discursive systems of knowledge, biophysical systems, and systems of technological autonomy. It is in thirty-year retrospect that *The Three Ecologies* appears to reach the status of theoretical clairvoyance, as Guattari's employment of a general ecological method forecasts the political rise of Donald Trump. For Guattari, the right-wing politician is recast as a form of mutant algae virally invading and expanding amid the posttruth social, technical, and material ecologies of late capitalism.

In looking to the Bateson quote that Guattari selected to open *The Three Ecologies,* an ecology of mind is described as a proscriptive method, which, given how American political history has played out since, could also be described as prophylactic: "There is an ecology of bad ideas, just as there is an ecology of weeds" (Bateson, as quoted in Guattari 1989, 131). Guattari's argument outlines how to critically diagnose the emergent destructive norms of capitalism's fixation on growth and overtaxation of the environment as toxic interactions by assuming a philosophical topology linking nature, culture, and technology: "The new ecological praxes," for Guattari, "articulate themselves across the whole range of these interconnected and heterogeneous fronts" (139). Ecological science is principally about mapping the interconnection of heterogeneous relations between the bounded systems of physical environments and organisms. Ecology, as a generalized critical method offered by Guattari following Bateson, instead recognizes how webs of subjective human thought and technological automation equally function according to models of cascade, succession, bioaccumulation, or the invasion of neighboring communities.

One critical difference lies in how Guattari (1989, 131) locates human thought and its social valence—which doesn't take the form of "subjects" but of "components of subjectification"—as just one interconnecting "ecology" that crosses and interacts with the two other ecological enclosures: the biophysical environment and the mechanical coevolution of technological forms. For the sake of comparison, the methodology of systemic discourse analysis would be a shallow version of what Guattari has in mind, as discourse privileges only the first ecology—the networked epistemology of minds in their individual and collective linguistic registers—while devaluing the composite influences of the latter two ecologies: operational effects between, and originating within, both the surrounding material environment and the ongoing phylogeny of machines.

The Three Ecologies posits a political theory for a world with increasingly visible environmental crises precipitated by the unchecked growth of capitalist economies, the widespread distribution of increasingly powerful technologies—like nuclear power—prone to novel geographical and temporal scales of ecological catastrophe, and those social algal blooms that seek to virally overpower competition to secure scarce resources. "We need to apprehend the world through the interchangeable lenses of the three ecologies," Guattari (1989, 134) writes,

for there are limits—as Chernobyl and AIDS have sav-
agely demonstrated—to the technico-scientific power
of humanity. Nature kicks back. If we are to orient the
sciences and technology toward more human goals, we
clearly need collective *management* and *control*—not blind
reliance on technocrats in the state apparatuses, in the
hope they will control developments and minimize risks in
fields largely dominated by the pursuit of profit. (emphasis added)

It's worth emphasizing that for Guattari, notwithstanding his
attempt to push political analysis past human language and
cognition, the human subject is primarily the emancipatory actor.
The goal of thinking across the *The Three Ecologies* involves the
"re-evaluat[ion] [of] the ultimate goal of work and human activities
in terms of criteria other than those of profit and productivity"
(Guattari 1989, 142) as the principal political vector for cultivating
sustainability across each ecological realm of analysis (semiotic,
biophysical, technological). Eschewing liberal individualism, Guattari's ecological politics advocate, in his terms, collective management and collective control—a vision akin to a socially radical and
transversal permaculture.

As demonstrated herein, Guattari specifically pivots on these
cybernetically inflected terms—*management* and *control*—in what
I see as a resigned acceptance of the ineluctability of the historical
concepts, and the corresponding institutional apparatuses, made
available by information theory, its cybernetic circulation, and
technological application. With such advocacy for collectivity, it is
individual faith in the technocratic and economic state administration of ecology under the superordinate guidance of profit and
productivity that proves the problem to be overcome by transversal reasoning across *The Three Ecologies.* Restated, environmental
politics become, How to think transversally about the reticulation
of the individual within the natural, technological, and social collective? How can collective control and management be achieved

apart from the overarching coordinate objectives of profit and streamlined productivity?

This chapter pauses on the notion of information as it shaped the concept of the ecosystem in postwar ecology. I trace the recursive history of the ecosystem as the idea originates in theories describing the mind as a system and subsequently becomes the dominant concept for describing biophysical reality as a cybernetic hybrid of nature and machine, otherwise, as an amalgamation of technological *and* ecological systems.[2] The informational paradigm authorizes Guattari's proposal for an intersystemic analysis of exchanges between mind, biophysical reality, and technology. Information supports a common theoretical ground for strategic conceptual fluidity between fields of study, as epitomized by the postwar appeal by the cybernetic technosciences to become a "universal discipline" through rhetorical strategies of "legitimacy exchange" (Bowker 1993, 116). This alleged universality between bounded disciplines is the epistemological conceit mimicked and exploited by Guattari in *The Three Ecologies.* Transversality is the revaluation of ecology as unnatural and technoecological, otherwise, as the acceptance of the total fusion of organism and machine conjured by the idealized image of the cybernetic ecosystem. Guattari amends the ecosystem with an elevated aim of political transformation as articulated from within a critical position assuming the systemic interactions of individual and collective psyche, natural processes, and the adjacent lives of machines: "The general ecology," as Erich Hörl (2013, 128) succinctly notes, "is an ecology of a natural–technical continuum."

I characterize Guattari's move to study the transversality between ecologies as an *immanent* critique that transgresses the enclosed epistemic boundaries of existing systems and disciplines. This move is *reluctant* insofar as Guattari recognizes that the informational paradigm that makes available and supports such a theoretical move equally enables the antipolitical formations that he argues against. This is evidenced by the ability for bad ideas to proliferate in technonatural media ecologies in a weedlike manner, as the perceived negative qualities of weeds follows a historical argument as opposed to an evolutionary one. Rhetorically, then, cybernetic universalism is recognized as ineluctable: as axiom, provocation, target, and tool. Guattari's critique confronts a system with systemic reason, which, as I describe throughout this chapter, is a recapitulation of the recursive problem that defines the politics of the ecosystem. Specifically, this chapter hones the efficacy of the ecosystem as a political term of media by highlighting the work the term does beyond its hybrid technonatural metaphorical status. Instead, the ecosystem is a *mechanism* that translates knowledge between two fields caught in the twentieth century's cybernetic fold: ecology and economy. This is most evident in the turn to eco-logical resilience-thinking in recent American environmental and military policy, as the convenient historical affinity found between ecology and economy under the aegis of the ecosystem is argued to rationalize the entrenched relationship between national secu-rity and resource extraction in a form of governance focused on tactical response to unpredictable, yet impending, ecological crisis.

Guattari (1989, 135) prophesized that in a media-informational environment, such as ours, politicians like "Donald Trump and his ilk—another form of algae—are permitted to proliferate unchecked." Despite the apparent prescience of this statement, I don't see value in reading Guattari's text for a preemptive and transversal explanation of the social support in Trump's 2016 election. Instead, I take another route and suggest that, accord-ing to the historical calibration of thought encapsulated by the ecosystem's strategic management of intellectual traffic between environmental, technological, and economic modes of organiza-tion, Guattari's text opens a theoretical path to understanding the Trump administration's environmental program as a strategy of governance *dependent* on the continuation of ecological crisis conditions. If Guattari highlights the challenge to thought posed by modern ecological crises that are anthropogenically economic and technological in origin, the list of "neoliberal catastrophes" that Nicole Shukin (2016) identifies as that *"to which we are becoming accustomed*: Fukushima, Deepwater Horizon, Chernobyl, Exxon Valdez, Bhopal, and so on," look to provide an ideal habitat for the "unchecked proliferation" of the Trump administration's mutated conservatism, which manifests in twinned environmental policies of ecological and economic *resilience.*

The following series of events appears heterogeneous but is, I maintain, identifiable as a part of the broader and unified ecosystemic governance embracing *resilience* planning:

> On June 6, 2016, President Trump suggested the addition of solar panels to greenwash and help finance the construction of the American border wall with Mexico, dovetailing xenophobia with sustainable energy investment and the Pentagon's strategic futurological work to forecast climate refugees from Mexico and Central America (Parenti 2011; Garfield 2017). In 2018, Interior Secretary Ryan Zinke launched a complementary initiative by retasking National Park Service officers to patrol the United States–Mexico border, citing migration as an "environmental disaster" (Green, 2018).

> On September 13, 2017, President Trump proposed corporate tax cuts via Twitter as the American humanitarian policy par excellence for hurricane-ravaged Puerto Rico (Klein 2017).

> On November 2, 2017, the Republican Party passed the Tax Cuts and Jobs Act, permitting Alaskan National Wildlife Refuge land sales to oil and natural gas companies. As a part of a broader policy move transforming environmentally protected reserves into financially active natural resource reserves, the inclusion of extreme energy extraction confirms the speculative efforts advanced by petrochemical corporations toward previously inaccessible arctic oil, which is made increasingly available by conditions consistent with climate change. This act is a clear move to *secure* and *securitize* a future when thawed ice

means both more drilling and less foreign energy depen- **59**
dence (Meiklejohn 2017; Hiltzik 2017; Jerving et al. 2015;
Lieberman and Rust 2015).

On February 12, 2018, President Trump's budget request
gestured toward realizing his campaign promise of an
American coal and nuclear renaissance. The marriage
of proposed coal and atomic energy growth confirms
an underrecognized alliance between revitalized investment in fossil fuel extraction, national security interest in
stockpiled materials for nuclear weapons and petroleum
for the military–industrial complex, and the continued
endorsement of a nuclear power transition as lauded by
neoliberal scientists, all while cutting renewable energy
initiatives (Cooper 2008, 42; Natter 2017; Gardner 2018).

Geoengineering is increasingly disseminated as "a techno-
utopian deus ex machina," but the idea originates in neoconservative think tanks already working to cast doubt
on climate change, as Philip Mirowski argues that manu-
factured ignorance itself is a stopgap measure intended
to preserve free market autonomy and economic growth
against ecological imperatives to the contrary (Mirowski,
Walker, and Abboud 2013; Mirowski 2013).

When considered through the following discussion, each of these
cynical prospects gains theoretical clarity with reference to the
history and mechanism of the ecosystem: *resilience,* otherwise,
how the state and economy adjust toward maintaining systemic
multidynamic cohesive stability by increasing financial gain and
enhancing national security upon encountering the uncertain, yet
imminent, destabilization promised by environmental threats.

Guattari was right: nature *has* become inseparable from culture,
but this critical observation is equally legible to those who would
exploit the entanglement. As the spokesperson for the Federal
Emergency Management Agency summed up the destructive
2017 hurricane season in the United States, "*the only way we*

become resilient as a nation is we have to create the true culture of preparedness among our citizenry" (Green 2017, emphasis added). As I conclude, cultures of resilience demonstrate why it is a mistake to think that the choreographed dance between neoliberal and neoconservative policies that specify the administration of environmental politics in the United States is a mode of governance ignorant to the imbrication of nature, culture, and technology.

Seeing environmental politics along Guattari's ecological topology, Matteo Pasquinelli (2017) works to expand the programmatic of "*machinic ecology*" to fully describe the historical cleavage of labor into energy (systemic material exchange) and information (energetic control). This series of bifurcations is part of an emerging environmental–governmental strategy that corresponds to three stages of capitalism and their complementary extractive machines. An "*epistemic rift*" forms "between energy and information that was provoked by industrial capitalism [the factory] and then amplified by cybernetics [ergonomic control society] and the digital revolution [planetary computation]" (312–13). He argues that the initial bifurcation was enacted during the onset of industrial capitalism by technologically organizing the productive force of labor into the extraction of natural resources, like coal (labor-become-energy), while the pedagogy of workers in the factory functioned as energetic control (information), as workers could then make use of the mined resources and autonomously operate extractive machines. For Pasquinelli (2017, 313), the large-scale machines of capitalism are diagrams describing how labor is breached into the historical abstractions of energy, or "labor as manual activity," and information, or "labor as a source of information that gives form to energy and matter." This "epistemic rift" replaces John Bellamy Foster's concept of "metabolic rift" recuperated from Karl Marx's study of the ecological fissure grown between humans as occupants of cities in industrial society and the natural soil conditions increasingly depleted by commercial agriculture and the accumulation of resources in large population centers (Foster 1999). Pasquinelli, instead, offers Guattari's "machinic ecology" as a method to diagnose the transactions of "*empirical assemblages*" that *link* both nature and society *through* the organized severance of labor into the abstractions of energy and information, as opposed to the traditional Marxian description of nature–society relations as rifting.

Pasquinelli proposes the "*machinic* [a]s indebted to the open framework inaugurated by cybernetics that aimed to dissolve the border between organic systems and technical systems" (324). Then, his advocacy of *machinic ecology* follows Guattari by employing the same informational paradigm that grounds both the potential and the problematic of the system, as the *machinic* rhetorically and strategically employs the openness of cybernetic universality to illuminate: "a mode of governance that attempts to dissolve labor conflicts into the fabric of information and energy, thus mystifying labor into technological forms so as to render it invisible" (313). As demonstrated in this chapter, the conceptual development of the ecosystem is central to the mode of governance implied by Pasquinelli, even, perhaps, going so far as to preempt and disarm Pasquinelli's ultimate recommendation that "it may be better to try and consolidate the assemblage of energy and information into new systemic notions" (321).

 Then, machinic ecology highlights the abstraction processes defining three stages of capitalist economic history (industrial, cybernetic, digital) alongside their corresponding machines, technologies, and institutions (factory, ergonomic control, computation) that give informational form to the matter produced by the energy of labor (312–13). As I compile here, there is an emerging set of political strategies centered on the ecosystem that follow the *epistemic rift* between energy and information by grounding conceptual exchanges between ecology and economy. Most dangerously, following Melinda Cooper and Jeremy Walker's (2012) genealogy of *resilience,* this mode of ecosystemic governance is positioned to gain from uncertain environmental conditions that are temporally and statistically inbound as future ecological crises precipitated by capitalist organization in the present.

Perhaps unsurprisingly, the concept of the ecosystem has a curious relationship to theories of the mind. As Laura Cameron recounts, British ecologist Arthur George Tansley's (1935) introduction of the term in the famous paper "The Use and Abuse of Vegetational Concepts and Terms" is partially indebted to his time undergoing psychoanalytic treatment with Sigmund Freud, twelve years previously. Tansley remained fascinated with Freud's theory and practice throughout his career, even laying out his own theory of mind in resemblance of his concept of the ecosystem: an "interwoven plexus of moving material . . . a more or less ordered system, or rather a system of systems . . . acting and reacting" (Tansley, quoted in Cameron 2004, 56). Cameron highlights how Tansley's original ecosystem aimed toward equilibrium asymptotically, similarly to Freud's theory of the psyche, which reveals the early ecosystem theory to be both an idealized model limited in application and a theory founded in relation to a constitutive negativity retaining an absence beyond the enclosure of the model.

Tansley's introduction of the term, and its logical proximity to contemporaneous theories of mind, is important for several reasons. As Cameron and Earley (2015, 479, 475) write, quoting Tansley, the ecosystem originally included the agency of human beings as the "most powerful biotic factor" under the banner of "*anthropogenic ecosystems* [which] differ from those developed independently of man." The early recognition and inclusion of human activity within scientific models of biophysical reality is crucial to environmental history because the term was later evacuated of this conceptual qualification in an explicit political application of the theory toward imperial ends during the Conservancy movement, which legitimated ecologists' role as "nature's managers" (Cameron and Earley 2015, 476) over an allegedly "de-peopled" wilderness. In this sense, the anthropocentric frame to the ecosystem—its recursive modeling of mind, agency, and nature—was repressed, as was Tansley's insistence, following Freud, that ecosystems strive toward was founded as a transversal object (physical system, mental, and environmental) in recursive epistemological relation to negativity.

Like many human and social sciences in the postwar period, ecology was an inheritor of the cybernetic program delineating the control exerted by information over energetic exchanges between humans, animals, and machines. In 1948, Yale ecologist G. Evelyn Hutchinson's interest in thinking together ecology and thermodynamic systems would unite Russian biogeochemist V. I. Vernadsky's approach to the "Biosphere," as a physical thermodynamic system composed of interacting living and inert matter, with Tansley's ecosystem through the introduction of the calculation of information as the control mechanism for the flow of energy in natural systems. After attending the interdisciplinary and influential Macy Conferences on cybernetics in 1948, following an invitation from Bateson, Hutchinson drew the "concept of circular causality as a means for describing the mechanisms by which ecological systems regulate themselves" (Bryant 2006, 66–67). In 1953, Eugene Odum synthesized these ideas into *Fundamentals of Ecology* by focusing and articulating a cybernetic ecosystem as a central model for theorizing nature as informational systems. Citing the influence of his brother Howard, who was a student of Hutchinson, the Odums's cybernetic ecology "swiftly became a dominant paradigm within the science, reaching its zenith with the International Biological Program in the late 1960s and early 1970s" (Bryant 2006, 71).

With the support of the Atomic Energy Commission, the Odums first worked to apply their concept of an ecosystem ecology in the 1950s by studying the circulation of radioactive isotopes leftover from U.S. nuclear weapons testing as the radiation passed through coral reef ecosystems.[3] The idea of a "secondary informational network" governing the material energetic exchanges in idealized biophysical systems through mechanisms of feedback linked both nature and technology in the same epistemology: "The grand laws which define the conditions of existence (gravity, conservation, dissipation, limiting factors, etc.) are all part of the informational network" (Odum and Patton, quoted in Bryant 2006, 88). This was one of the first steps in conceptually reconceiving the whole Earth as a whole system (Bryant 2006), but importantly, it is not the only one linked to the geopolitical *urgency* of nuclear weapons development, as Paul Edwards (2012) and Joseph Masco (2010, 2017) have noted regarding the theoretical, technological, and cultural links between atmospheric atomic testing and the computation of climatic complexity. The Odums theory maintained that certain machines and ecosystems were equivalent on the grounds of the cybernetic position that self-regulating systems are universal, but how this term—*ecosystem*—informs an epistemological relationship between economy and ecology within an informational paradigm requires further clarification.

Ecosystem as Apparatus

In effect, as William Harold Bryant (2006, 57) comments on the critical historical reception of the postwar ecosystem, "cybernetics turned ecology into a technoscience." While Bryant's project is to recuperate the history of the term as central to then burgeoning twentieth-century environmental political movements and the conceptual distinction between destructive and green technologies, Fred Turner (2006, 2010) has argued that the interdisciplinary import of cybernetic whole-system holism into liberal political movements in California (especially environmentalism) laid the foundations for the individualizing ideology of the network society that drove Silicon Valley commercialism. (This is not to mention the ecologically devastating demattering of hardware from software that drove the emergence of e-waste; Gabrys 2013.) Turner's critique, by way of Geoffrey Bowker (as cited in Turner 2006, 25), draws out how the "cybernetic rhetoric" of "legitimacy exchange" encapsulates a strategic "process by which experts in one area draw on the authority of experts in another area to justify their activities." Bernard Geoghegan (2011) has furnished these "politics of knowledge" with an account of how the heterogeneous relationship between the mutability of concepts in the cybernetic sciences accord to a set of nondiscursive "instruments and techniques" accompanying the conceptual development of these fields. For this task, Geoghegan adapts the term Michel Foucault used to describe the set of strategic relations between a discourse and its heterogeneous, generalized material implementation: *dispositif* (96–98).

Geoghegan's alteration—"the cybernetic apparatus"—is appealing in its deliberate conflation of Foucault's use of the French words *dispositif,* "a strategic system of relations established among a heterogonous ensemble," and *appareil,* "which may connote an instrument or tool" (Geoghegan 2011, 99). As he continues, the melding of the two terms in the English "apparatus"

> poetically realizes that peculiar *disunity-in-unity* that characterizes Foucault's use of the term *dispositif.* Moreover, this exploitation of semantic dislocation thematizes a kind of productive terminological slippage between languages and disciplines that was the condition of possibility for the cybernetic apparatus. (99–100, emphasis added)

Geoghegan's description of the cybernetic apparatus is crucial, especially as the term fully embraces as constitutional the twofold ambiguity of cybernetic history: fool's errand efforts to find a unified metaphysical logic for the "disunity and heterogeneity . . . that constituted cybernetics's peculiar strength and attraction" while giving a fuller account for the nondiscursive technologies and institutions that usually "disappears from the historical picture and is replaced by hermeneutics and language" (100–101). As Foucault defined the term's deployment while defending *The History of Sexuality* (Foucault 1978) from a panel of prominent psychoanalytic theorists, *dispositif* intends "a thoroughly heterogeneous ensemble" that forms "at a given historical moment that of responding to an *urgent need.* . . . Its general form is both discursive and nondiscursive" (Foucault 1980, 194–95, 197). For Geoghegan, Cold War geopolitics supplies the *urgent* establishment of strategic heterogeneous relations that form the cybernetic apparatus.

The ecosystem—as a cybernetic distributary—also satisfies Foucault's criteria under similar duress. This is especially the case as a longer etymology of ecosystem gives this particular avenue of the cybernetic apparatus a privileged relationship to the nondiscursive processes of biophysical reality. This privilege—the ecosystem's purview of environment—is inherited from the translational mechanism founded on the historic conceptual connections between ecology and economy, later repressed and packaged for use by cybernetic universalism.

The Ecosystem Apparatus: Why Management?

Refining the conceptual relationship between ecology and economy—and the ecosystem's work as a translator between the two—benefits from an etymological detour. In Reinhold Martin's history identifying how former American president Richard Nixon's alleged environmental policies—including the establishment of the Environmental Protection Agency—complemented his economic positions in the 1970s, he outlines "the origins of the term *ecology* in the Greek *oikos,* meaning 'house' or 'home,' which also forms the root of *economy,* with the two terms translating etymologically as the 'study' and the 'management' of the 'household'" (Martin 2004, 82). This exchange between ecology and economy is visible in the *urgent* historical context of the increased media visibility of American environmental crises precipitated by Fordist industrial capitalism without ecological regulation. Nixon's environmental protection assuaged public concerns following the critique enabled by the ecosystem's use throughout Paul Ehrlich's (1968) *The Population Bomb,* Barry Commoner's (1972) *The Closing Circle,* and the Club of Rome's *The Limits to Growth* (Meadows et al. 1972). This is not to mention the observable deteriorating conditions of the American landscape described in Rachel Carson's ([1962] 2002) *Silent Spring,* or the novel spectacle of polluted rivers and lakes catching fire in Ohio holding an emblematic visual analogy with the state violence of napalm weaponry use in Vietnam.

As Martin recounts, in 1971, Nixon suspended "the convertibility
of the dollar into gold or other reserves" (Nixon, quoted in Martin
2004, 93) and made this full repeal of the gold standard—
abstracting capital from materiality—permanent in part due to
the 1973 energy crisis precipitated by the OPEC oil embargo. This
history cynically betrays those nondiscursive instruments and
institutions established in the fluid exchange between economy
and ecology: the delinking of currency from materiality enabled
new and virtually ungrounded financial practices, including "the
speculative exchange of statistical *risk*," and futures derivative trading, inclusive of environmental risk (Martin 2004, 94). This is clearly
a politically strategic action in line with the *epistemic rift* grown
between energy and information. Meanwhile, the emergence of the
Environmental Protection Agency (EPA) as an institution that corresponds to the identification of "an outer limit to the exploitation of
the external physical environment" reveals the same institution as
a political smokescreen for the economic "compensat[ion] on the
inside, at the semiotic level of capital-as-such" (Martin 2004, 95–96).
In other words, the complementary traffic between ecology and
economy—protection and abstraction—recapitulates the Greek
origins of the management of the household, here conceived as
the relation between external (ecological) and internal (economic)
management respectively.

In Giorgio Agamben's pursuit of an etymological definition for
Foucault's *dispositif,* he lands in similar territory: "Now, what is
the translation of the fundamental Greek term [*oikonomia*] in the
writings of the Latin Fathers? *Dispositio.* The Latin term *dispositio,*
from which the French term *dispositif,* or apparatus, derives, comes
therefore to take on the complex semantic sphere of the theological *oikonomia*" (Agamben 2009, 11). Agamben continues to define
apparatus—which is linked by Martin to the relation between
ecology and economy—as a declension of the theological *oikonomia,* otherwise "a set of practices, bodies of knowledge, measures,
and institutions that aim to manage, govern, control, and orient—in
a way that purports to be useful—the behaviors, gestures, and

thoughts of human beings" (12). Through *oikonomia* as *dispositif,* ecology and economy find their way back to the indirect governmental production of the subject.

Then, recalling one of the questions that opened this chapter— what is ecological inquiry's distinct relationship to the nondiscursive realms of technological and biophysical reality?—Agamben gives us the sketch of an answer via his interpretation of Foucault's *dispositif.* This is to say that Agamben (2009) responds by linking *dispositif* to a much older philosophical question regarding the establishment of positive governance through theological institutions: "the set of beliefs, rules, and rites that in a certain society and at a certain historical moment are externally imposed on individuals . . . the administration of the *oikos* (the home) and, more generally, management" (4, 8). This gives a partial explanation for why Foucault offers a secular version of technological and institutional governance through power's mediation of historical knowledge formations, however, Foucault's terms are more specific: "the *episteme* is a specifically *discursive* apparatus, whereas the apparatus in its general form is both discursive and non-discursive" (Foucault 1978, 197). Like the ecosystem's theoretical blend of natural, technical, and anthropogenic activity, for Foucault, the *dispositif* is an operational description of both *discursive and nondiscursive* factors. Then, when Agamben reasons that *dispositif* comes to occupy a more general and developed mechanism analogous to *positivité* in Foucault's (as cited in Agamben 2009, 3) archaeological theories of the 1960s, he mistakenly sells the role of the nondiscursive (biology, ecology, technology, institutional, etc.) short. So far, then, governance through the positive, strategically urgent, and ancillary managerial strategies of *oikonomia* becomes *dispositif* for Agamben. For Foucault, however, the association between *oikonomia* and *dispositif* produces a more complex theorization of governance than what is glossed by Agamben. Given the etymological proximity of both *economy* and *ecology (oikonomia)* to *dispositif,* a fuller consideration of how nondiscursive activity factors into Foucault's terminology will demonstrate why Agamben's reading falters in this regard.

Agamben misses a crucial part of this picture that proves central to my argument that the ecosystem is an apparatus. In an essay titled "What an Apparatus Is Not," Pasquinelli (2015) provides a compelling counterhistory to Agamben's question while moving beyond etymological convenience to give a complete account of the emergence of the *dispositif* concept. By looking to Foucault's first use of the term during the lectures on the abnormal at the Collège de France in 1975, Pasquinelli discovers the term's genesis in the holistic organicism of German *Naturphilosophie.* This is, not coincidentally, the intellectual environment within which the word *ecology* emerges in 1866, according to Ernst Haeckel's development of Charles Darwin's phrase "economy of nature—the investigation of the total relations of the animal both to its inorganic and its organic environment" (Haeckel, quoted in Golley 1993, 2, 207).

Pasquinelli argues that Foucault's term can be traced to a constellation of sources that gives *dispositif* a renewed political interpretation in its possibility to recuperate the autonomy of the organic subject. The primary source for *dispositif* is not a theological tradition but Foucault's doctoral advisor, Georges Canguilhem, who drew the term into sharp relief across three texts: *Essai sur quelques problèmes concernant le normal et le pathologique* (Canguilhem 1943); "Machine and Organism" (Canguilhem [1952] 2008); and the second edition of *The Normal and the Pathological* with an appended section titled "augmenté de Nouvelles réflexions concernant le normal et le pathologique" (Canguilhem [1966] 1991), which significantly adds reflection to the relationship between organicism and social theory, critiquing the concepts of organic unity that drove nationalist ideologies during World War II.

In sum, Canguilhem develops his definition of *normativity* from neurologist Kurt Goldstein's theory of the organism, for which

> *normative power* is the ability of each organism (and spe-
> cifically of the human brain) to invent, modify and destroy
> its own norms, internal and external habits, rules and

behaviors, in order to adapt better to its own *Umwelt* (or surrounding environment), particularly in cases of illness and traumatic incidents and in those conditions that challenge the survival and unity of the organism. (Pasquinelli 2015, 7)

Canguilhem's admiration for Goldstein lies in the observation that the organism is a system of internal systems aiming toward dynamic equilibria all while in constant antagonism with the external environment. (In the revised portion of *The Normal and the Pathological* that regards social theory, equilibria of systems becomes "homeostasis"; Canguilhem 1991, 253, 260.)

In this sense, when the organism experiences a shock, it is able to amplify existing, or develop entirely new, norms (perceived retroactively as abnormal symptoms of illness) to compensate for disruption and correct the system. Canguilhem, following Goldstein, views the "abnormal as a manifestation of a positive normative process itself" (Pasquinelli 2015, 7). It is in this light that Pasquinelli sees Canguilhem's enduring thesis as a description of an organic "normative *dispositif*" (13):

it is the historical anteriority of the future abnormal which gives rise to a normative intention. The normal is the effect obtained by the execution of the normative project, it is the norm exhibited after the fact. . . . Consequently it is not paradoxical to say that the abnormal, while logically second, is existentially first. (Canguilhem 1991, 243)

Organic life is the autonomous biological development of new norms in response to externally encountered conditions rocking a normal state. New norms are perceived as abnormal due to the a posteriori effect of normalization: a process that spurs diagnostic response according to the normative intention that counterintuitively follows the perception of abnormality. The subsequent redefinition of the normal—through the categorical pathologization of the abnormal—returns the system to homeostasis from the shock delivered via encounter with the changing external environment,

now with difference: "Thus, the organism is always *in-becoming.*
Truly 'sick' is instead the organism that is incapable of invention
and experimentation of new norms: the organism that is, para-
doxically, not capable of making mistakes" (Pasquinelli 2015, 7). As
I imply later, it is precisely such a "true sickness" that plagues the
adaptation-oriented policies of ecological resilience.

Pasquinelli, then, mines Canguilhem's influence to give a clearer
account of two distinct, yet interdependent, definitions of *dispositif*
in Foucault: one nondiscursive in its distribution through the
technological and institutional operations of indirect power, or "the
'organic' incarnation of power into an impersonal infrastructure of
procedures, standards, and norms," and a second corresponding
dispositif guiding the "power of normalization" that characterizes
"the autonomous production of the categories of the normal and
the pathological by state apparatuses" (Pasquinelli 2015, 10).
This dynamic interplay is, in fact, easily identified in an ecological
reading of Foucault.

Normalization is a crucial process in *Discipline and Punish* (Foucault
1977). The *origins* of disciplinary power—often attributed to Jeremy
Bentham's diagram of the Panopticon—are instead more loosely
identified as a distribution of social institutions and technologies
established during the onset of plague management in European
cities:

> the plague as a form, at once real and imaginary, of *disor-
> der* had as its *medical and political correlative discipline* . . .
> the functioning of an extensive power that bears in a dis-
> tinct way over all individual bodies—this is the Utopia of a
> perfectly governed city. The plague (envisaged as a pos-
> sibility at least) is the trial in the course of which one may
> define ideally the exercise of disciplinary power. (Foucault
> 1977, 198, emphasis added)

As Foucault scales the normative operation of Canguilhem's
autonomous organism to that of disciplinary power as a plasm
finely distributed throughout individuals and institutions within a

society, the plague as external, environmental, and at-the-time-illegible threat of unperceivable disease gave rise to a new set of responsive disciplinary norms: quarantine, confinement, visible enclosure, and, most importantly, the beginning of statistical population censuses. For Foucault, it was plague that occasioned "surveillance . . . based on a system of permanent registration. . . . The registration of the pathological must be constantly centralized" (Foucault 1977, 196).

These new norms established in response to plague were initially abnormal social projections *through which* a new order of normal was subsequently defined as pathology. The social organism encountering disease *as disorder* returns to homeostasis with the *medical and political correlative of discipline.* Now, an immunitary social is better prepared for future shock with both a sense of normality via the pathological and those normalizing institutions prepared for subsequent encounters with environmental instability. Pasquinelli argues that this disunity-in-unity passing *between* individuals, technology, and the social whole discloses the returned specter of organicism: "As in the nightmares of the worst German *Staatsbiologie,* Foucault's power apparatuses appear to cast the shadow of a gigantic macro-organism of which we would not dare to think" (Pasquinelli 2015, 14). It is Foucault's social *interpretation* of Canguilhem's organic *dispositif*—and Foucault's consequential hint of superorganic social unity—that sets up the terms for Pasquinelli's ecological–political intervention.

First, to recap, this chapter has traced the concept of the ecosystem from its proximal origins to a psychoanalytic theory of mind, through to its cybernetic reinvention in the postwar period, and its contiguity with Foucault's notion of *dispositif*—both etymologically (*oikonomia,* alongside ecology and economy) and in terms of intellectual heritage (Canguilhem's encounter with German biophilosophy). Then, I have demonstrated how *dispositif* contains an ecological dimension through both a relationship to the nondiscursive (generalized governance through institutions and technologies) and a relationship to environment specifically (ecology as the study

of management between interior economy and exterior environment, and, strategies of normative organic autonomy responding
to external disturbance acting on internal systems of organization
that aim toward homeostasis). When Pasquinelli (2017, 318–19)
states that "cybernetics was the *normative project* of power in the
age of information machines—a shift that Michel Foucault . . . failed
to record in his epistemology of power" (emphasis added), he
implicitly recognizes the descriptive limits of *dispositif* as it holds a
twofold definition (positive governance and organic social normalization). This clears ground to pursue *dispositif* as more fully in line
with Geoghegan's English reformulation of the word: the disunity-
in-unity functionality of *the cybernetic apparatus.*

Pasquinelli's provocative statement about the twentieth-century
cybernetic control society being the archive enclosing Foucault's
analysis is an argument supported by two compatible studies. First,
one year before his full articulation of the "Postscript on Control
Societies" (Deleuze [1990] 1995), Deleuze ([1989] 1995, 344–45)
remarked in "What Is a *Dispositif*?" that "the disciplines Foucault described are the history of what we are slowly ceasing to be and our
current *apparatus* is taking shape in attitudes of open and constant
control" (emphasis added). Second, Céline Lafontaine (2007, 36)
more explicitly sees Foucault's thought as implicitly reflective of the
contemporaneous "*Zeitgeist*" of informational control: "In defining
power as a system of relations and emphasizing its discursive
nature, Foucault is well and truly in line with the cybernetic rupture. . . . Depoliticized, decentralized and totalized, the concept of
power as developed by Foucault is strangely similar to cybernetic
control." The implications of Pasquinelli, Deleuze, and Lafontaine,
taken together, substantiate Pasquinelli's (2017, 314) imperative for
"a new critique of cybernetics [that] should help to remind us of the
role of information in the growth of the old industrial apparatus."
It is at this precise point between the dislocation of energy and
information, economy and ecology, that I situate the ecosystem as
a term describing the historical normative apparatuses critically
taken up by Guattari's call for collective management and control.

The ecosystem as apparatus is a heterogeneous coordination of relations between mind, environment, and machine that respond to conditions of historical urgency, as is evident in nondiscursive governmental institutions, techniques, technologies, and the normalizing position of the adaptive social whole disposed toward future environmental crisis. This reading of ecosystem is further supported by one major historical outcome of the concept and its institutional application through ecological and economic *resilience.*

Autonomy in the Organicist Ecosystem

It is worth recalling that Tansley's introduction of the ecosystem concept was a direct response to the primacy of organicism in ecology. The "superorganism" and "complex organism" were the dominant metaphors in the 1930s, when "plants that comprised the superorganism worked together as interacting parts, and the community as a whole maintained itself in dynamic equilibrium within the shifting conditions of its environment by means of physiological processes" (Bryant 2006, 44–45). Tansley identified a problem within the field that the ecosystem redressed: on one hand, "superorganism" and "complex organism" evangelized holism and emergence "that created for ecology the same problems as did vitalism: an orientation toward untestable, unempirical explanations for idealized constructs" (46), while on the other hand, previous models reducing organic complexity to "the mechanistic actions of molecules" missed the functionality of how many parts "worked together to maintain the integrity of the whole" (33). Then, the utility of the ecosystem concept was located within how

> living things lost their privileged status and became, along with non-living matter, mutually formative components of a larger, encompassing entity. The ecosystem concept oriented ecology toward process and dynamics and away from taxonomy and natural history; toward the particular and the material, and away from the ideal and unverifi-

able. In so doing, it circumvented the mechanist-vitalist binary by providing a rigorously materialist, empirical way to address wholes without reducing their complexity. (48)

By 1942, Raymond Lindeman had published a quantifiable study of solar energy passing through a lake ecosystem as physicochemically processed by "producers," "consumers," and "decomposers" (Bryant 2006, 48). It was this conceptual movement toward the quantifiable study of energy within a thermodynamically modeled physical–natural system, constituted by interacting "biotic and abiotic components" (48), that primed the ecosystem for its reception in the cybernetic sciences. The introduction of information feedback, as the control mechanism for energy transfer, gave a theoretical framework that accounted for self-regulation in a given idealized biophysical system.

Just as Tansley appeared suspicious of organicism in ecology, so is Pasquinelli of this impulse in Foucault. Canguilhem's theory of the abnormal—and its critical social application to normative French institutions—crystallized specifically within postwar France due to heightened recognition of the "dangers of *organicism*" that Pasquinelli (2015, 11–12) defines as "the metaphors that were born in the biological sciences and then clumsily transplanted into the political sciences." This is the case, he maintains, because Canguilhem was at the time fully aware of how "German *Naturphilosophie,* from Kant to Goethe, from Humboldt to Haeckel, from Driesch to Uexküll, is built up around the organic unity of the living, which is then delivered 'hands tied' to political philosophy and legal theory" (12). Implied here is an intellectual mistranslation bluntly shuttled from *Naturphilosophie*—including Haeckel's ecology—directly into social theorization, contributing toward the "organicist paradigm [that] led German society to drift, eventually, into the catastrophe of Nazism" (13).

Canguilhem, for Pasquinelli, offered a careful philosophical distinction that challenged the organicist perspective maintaining an easy application of the procedure of the normative to social happenings and institutions. "The organism is formed around an *internal environment* of organs that can grow but not significantly change their configuration," yet "society [i]s an *external disposition* of machine-organs that often extend and accumulate against each other," meaning that the individual and the technological/institutional implementation of the social "evolve in a completely different way" (12). The organism and social technologies/institutions evolve *in completely different ways.* Pasquinelli concludes that Foucault's inheritance of the *dispositif* loses Canguilhem's insistence that "the social organization is able to *invent new organs* that are no longer an imitation of nature but follow its sense of production," as Foucault instead reversed: "the normative autonomy of the subject and, specifically, technology as a potentiality of the living" (12, 11). Foucault's alteration of his advisor's thesis formulates "knowledge as an *expression of power upon life*" rather than "knowledge as an *expression of life,*" thereby withdrawing the "normative *potentia*" (13) of the organism to articulate the full theorization of power found in the dual (nondiscursive and normative) *dispositif.* Hence Foucault maintains a hint of the superorganic unity in the *dispositif* that Canguilhem so carefully sought to avoid. It is Pasquinelli's intervention to imply critical value in the conceptual distinction between the organic autonomy of the subject and the organic autonomy of the machine—a crucial difference easily effaced in the dynamics of the theorization of power as circulating and accumulating in populations, institutions, and technologies.

This intellectual history is important because it runs parallel to a series of conceptual movements coupling the organic to the political as filtered through the twentieth-century cybernetic ecosystem. In the 1960s and 1970s, James Lovelock was studying the possibility of life on Mars while working for NASA. Drawing knowledge from cybernetic ecosystem theory that maintained that biophysical reality worked as a materially closed, energetically open whole system governed by informational self-regulation, Lovelock reasoned that since "Earth's air was full of reactive gases of biological origin," then "the composition of the atmosphere in fact depended upon the life on its surface" (Bryant 2006, 229). Following a xenobiological line of inquiry, Lovelock determined that NASA didn't need to visit Mars to ascertain whether the planet hosted organic life. He could deduct that answer based on observing the Martian atmosphere by telescope from Earth, as theoretically understanding the composition of an atmosphere as being part of a system composed of interacting biotic (if present) and abiotic factors supported the inference that a planet's lifeless character would be reflected in spectral analysis of the chemical makeup of the given atmosphere. If Mars had organic life, you should be able to see its effects on a planetary scale.

Lovelock (1995, 10) returned this observation to the planet Earth in his durable thesis, the "Biocybernetic Universal System Tendency/ Homeostasis," which maintained,

> Life on Earth shaped and determined the physical com-
> position of the planet, just as the physical planet shaped
> and determined that character of life. . . . Life exists
> planet-wide or not at all. . . . The quantity and distribu-
> tion of organisms would need to be sufficient to regulate
> the planetary environment and keep it comfortable for
> living things. . . . Species do not merely adapt, through
> evolution, to the environment they find themselves in.
> They continually change their physical and chemical envi-
> ronment. Species and environment co-evolve in an indi-
> visible process. . . . Viewed as a whole integrated system,
> *the Earth could be considered a single living organism in its*
> *own right.* . . . It was self-organizing and self-regulating;
> through cybernetic circuits of negative feedback, the
> planet maintained itself in dynamic equilibrium, just as an
> individual organism maintains homeostasis. (Bryant 2006,
> 229–30, emphasis added)

After receiving the advice of his friend and neighbor, author William Golding, Lovelock (1995, vii) renamed his idea of a self-regulating and complex unity "Gaia."

Then, what makes a planetary-scale Gaian superorganism different from more traditional organicist notions? Complexity and disequilibrium. Beginning in the late 1970s and building momentum through the 1980s, the idea of complexity had profound implications for both the ecological and economic sciences. Looking at Gaia, what Lovelock made clear was that Earth's history of life did not diminish in biological difference according to an entropic propulsion toward the heat death of equilibria. Rather, life responds to thresholds of disequilibria by progressing toward an increasingly complex diversity of forms that regulate the abiotic and material imbalances that support the conditions for the phenomenon of life itself. As Melinda Cooper (2008, 35) explains regarding Lovelock's conceptual move from the thermodynamic planetary evolutionary model of the biosphere to one of complexity, as illustrated by Gaia, "life, in this view, is intrinsically expansive—its field of stability is neither rigorously determined nor constant. . . . Its law of evolution is one of increasing complexity rather than entropic decline, and its specific creativity is autopoietic rather than adaptive." Biospheric self-regulation was located within the regenerative capacities of life in its interrelating variety, and more specifically, microbial life was highlighted as the most crucial component in the system given its ability to reanimate in the most extreme geographies.

Cooper argues that Gaia theory is a part of a broader and, again, disunified-yet-unified *ecological* response that folded alongside an *economic* cooptation. She locates the traffic of this ecosystemic apparatus in the reaction to the restrictive theoretical and political challenges posed by environmental steady-state advocacy, like the Club of Rome's *Limits to Growth* (Meadows et al. 1972) and *Beyond the Limits: Global Collapse or a Sustainable Future* (Meadows et al. 1992). Upon comprehending the consequences of how 97 percent of industrial production was dependent on nonrenewable fossil fuel extraction, the imperative offered by then-nascent degrowth environmental perspectives maintained that "the earth is finite. . . . Limits to growth . . . were time-like rather than space-like. This meant that we might have already gone beyond the threshold at

which an essential resource such as oil could be sustainably con-
sumed, long before we would notice its actual depletion" (Cooper
2008, 17). The Club of Rome had concluded after two studies that
capitalist economic growth could not outstrip the material ecological equilibria of the planet without encountering catastrophe.
It followed that solid-state economies were mandatory to stave
off collapse, as plans to continue neglecting the limits operated in
ignorance that "we were already living beyond the limit, in a state
of suspended crisis, innocently waiting for the future to boomerang
back in our faces" (Cooper 2008, 17). Rather than act on the Club
of Rome's prescription, and in accordance with the ecosystemic
drive of "capitalist delirium" (Cooper 2008, 21) that reestablishes
the ordinates of growth and accumulation in the bald-faced reality
of scarcity, the entwined limits to both life (ecology) and capital
(economy) needed to be invented and reinvented so as to *promise*
a future both livable *and* returnable. The promise, of course, was
not offered to everyone.

Cooper (2008) uses the term *bioeconomy* to describe the codevel-
opment of the twentieth-century turn in economic, earth-system,
and life sciences toward complexity, as each field responded to
theories proposing limits to growth as though in concert. For Lovelock, Lynn Margulis, and Dorion Sagan, "their rereading of evolution
thus concludes with certitude that microbial life will outsurvive all
limits to growth—certainly it will outsurvive the human race and
quite possibly the end of the earth" (Cooper 2008, 39). In a political
indictment of how the coherent philosophy of Lovelock's Gaia
hypothesis was mistranslated into a series of neoliberal economic
policies and institutions, the idea that the planet was an autopoietic living system capable of self-regulation and autonomous
sustainability gave ground to rationalize strategies of financial
biospeculation intended to stave off a meaningful divestment from
oil. Cooper writes,

> [Biosphere science, complexity science, and related theo-
> ries] may well have their origins in essentially revolution-
> ary histories of the earth . . . , but in the current context

they are more likely to lend themselves to distinctly neoliberal antienvironmentalism. . . . Whether this is a misinterpretation of complexity theory, at odds with the intentions of the theorists themselves, is in a sense beside the point, since in the absence of any substantive critique of political economy, any philosophy of *life as such* runs the risk of celebrating *life as it is.* And the danger is only exacerbated in a context such as ours, where capitalist relations have so intensively invested in the realm of biological reproduction. . . . It is because life is neguentro-pic, it seems, that economic growth is without end. And it is because life is self-organizing that we should reject all state regulation of markets. This is a vitalism that comes dangerously close to equating the evolution of life with capital. (41–42)

On one side of the mistranslation, contradictory theories of ecological modernization and green capitalism introduced the imperative to grow capitalist economies to the tune of sustainability, only to end up making unachievable promises beyond the limits. On another side, environmental regulation was repudiated with the charge of anthropomorphism, as Cooper identifies Lovelock's continued endorsement of nuclear power as a symptom of the anti-humanism present in the most drastic interpretation of Gaia: does Earth truly need humans—or all humans—to survive? Probably not, as long as the microbes will.

Cooper's theory poses a difficult problem: while complexity and its various incarnations yield a refined image of the planet's mechanisms, history shows us that there are those who deliberately exploit that knowledge in bad faith of the stated aspirations of good science. By acknowledging the philosophical coherence of Earth as a complex system, the question gets turned around: rather than hold a theory of life responsible for its inheritors, what instead is required of critique to meet *the life of ideas* on political grounds? As a methodological inspiration, I advance the ecosystem as the conceptual ground supporting exchanges between natural and economic science. The ecosystem is a mechanism for such exchanges as facilitated by the disunity-in-unity inherited from the cybernetic apparatus.

Economists and policy makers from the Carter and Reagan administrations through to the Clinton and Bush governments formulated responsive positions to the determination of limits to growth by proposing speculative economies drawn from knowledge in the life sciences. In one compelling example, citing George W. Bush's "notoriously antienvironmental" regime, Cooper (2008, 47) illustrates how his Department of Energy's Office of Science in 2004 "adopt[ed] a language that recalls the Gaia hypothesis as much as the more economistic calculations of ecological modernization [by looking] to the history of microbial and biospheric evolution as a source of future solutions to the looming energy crisis [and] plac[ing] special emphasis on the potential industrial applications of extremophiles." Gaia's foundational interest in life's capacity for regeneration in the most extreme geographies begins to look like some of the promised fallback fantasies intended to move economic development past limits projected regarding the scarcity of nonrenewable resources. After years of implementing and institutionalizing such strategies, Cooper argues that we're now well beyond the limits and waiting for the boomerang. But this isn't the most frightening prospect. The indirect consequence of such avid assurance of growth-past-the-limits is the preparation of a new set of cynical strategies: the imagination of the production of surplus value from an industrially scorched earth. Otherwise, how can surplus be extracted from a future that assumes that life will continue to grow in the ruins of capitalism?

Financing the Whole Earth as a Whole System

Truth is stranger than fiction, as one such financial imaginary emerges in the evolving transactions of the cybernetic apparatus-become-ecosystem. In 1984, during fears of nuclear apocalypse and the emergent dream of escaping the planet to off-world colonies in preservation of growing populations and industry, the private research corporation Space Biospheres Ventures started to consolidate an experimentally sustainable commune into a series of tests. These were outwardly capitalist endeavors to develop patents for space habitats in the isolation of the Arizona desert. The tests led to the establishment of Biosphere 2: an enclosed, self-regulating ecosystem designed to support human, animal, and plant life without any material exchange with, or external reliance upon, Biosphere 1—planet Earth.

The experiment took cues from Princeton physicist Gerard O'Neill's proposal that self-regulating space colonies were a viable technoecological solution to the perceived global population crisis and the apparent limit to an expanding society's dependence on oil and accordingly turbulent geopolitics. The three-acre enclosure cost $200 million and is the world's largest ecological experiment, funded by a Texan oil magnate named Ed Bass. While Biosphere 2, over the various experiments it ran, ended up producing a large amount of valuable climate change research since its beginnings in the early 1990s, Peder Anker (2017, 125) recounts that the project had less utopian motivations than its stated goal of simulating a space colony: "The aim of the Biosphere 2 was also to build a shelter in which Bass and his friends could survive in co-evolution with thousands of other species in case the eco-crisis turned Biosphere 1 into a dead planet like Mars [and t]hey believed that 'Glass Ark' could secure their personal survival while at the same time rescue some of the world's biodiversity."

The history of this project is well covered elsewhere,[4] but recent political events have shaped the importance of Biosphere 2. The presence of Alt-right spokesman and former advisor to President Trump Steve Bannon as an intermittent financial administrator for the project between 1991 and 1994 merits a brief consideration in light of how Cooper sees the mistranslation of Gaia's ecosystemic vitalism as key to understanding emergent strategies of speculative investment. As recently reported, part of Bannon's interest in

the project was premised on its failure. After the second wave of
scientists were evacuated from the enclosure, Bannon used the
heightened CO_2 levels that were consistent with modeled expectations of a world undergoing anthropogenic climate change "to
measure how quickly commercially harvested trees would grow in
a carbon dioxide–rich atmosphere" (Niiler 2016). "[The trees] shot
right up" (Niiler 2016), said Tony Burgess, a botanist working there
at the time. In Bannon's eyes, Biosphere 2 became commercially
viable as a pilot plant for how to make money from climate change.
This is a glimpse of an economic investment strategy literally bank-
ing on the failure of planet Earth. Once visible as the whole system
of Biosphere 1, the Earth's anthropogenic climate also enters the
financial system. Dipesh Chakrabarty (2009, 22) has influentially
argued that "climate change, refracted through global capital, will
no doubt accentuate the logic of inequality that runs through the
rule of capital," yet "there are no lifeboats here for the rich and the
privileged."[5] In final recognition that the limits of growth come with
a price, Chakrabarty's thesis is challenged by Bannon's Biosphere
and those who seek to finance the time that remains.[6]

In their shared perspective on the dangers posed by theories of
life articulated in the absence of a critique of political economy,
I see Pasquinelli and Cooper as compatible in diagnosing such
ecological–political problems that result from the ecosystem
apparatus's merger of ecology and economy. As Cooper (2008, 49)
suggests, responding to such historical interdisciplinary translations involves an "effective ecological counterpolitics" that attends
to the delirious drive to model future worlds while destroying them
in the present under the assumption of maintaining the deleterious
status quo—the delirium that characterizes "[our] living on the
cusp between petrochemical and biospheric modes of accumulation, the foregone conclusion of oil depletion and the promise
of bioregeneration." This counterpolitics requires "work in the
prospective mode, to detect and preempt the new forms of scarcity
that are being built into the promise of a bioregenerative economy"
(49–50). In the case of Bannon's Biosphere modeling the surplus

profit to be gained from a world undergoing slow but predictable anthropogenic change, the prospect of serious climate mitigation appears forgone as the continuation of fossil fuel denominated industrial production is assumed. Critique needs to continue with Cooper's temporal position in mind: who is lining up to finance the conditions of continued growth in an anthropogenic future?

In a complementary position, Pasquinelli offers a philosophical account for the renewed potential of social technologies by way of Canguilhem's careful positioning toward organicism, a concept that appears alongside the prospective surplus value exposed by a Gaian planet. Pasquinelli (2015, 12) sees political possibility, like Guattari, in technology as developed aside from capitalism, but technology must be considered as clearly distinct from the patterns of organic autonomy: "I propose to call *biomorphism* that mode in which *life does not imitate itself,* but is projected into the *ab*-normal social relations, mutant relations of production and further planes of consistency without looking back." His conceptual distinction most clearly illustrates the need to divorce the ecological study of life from the economic study of material governance, coordinated as they are within the ecosystem apparatus.

While subjective organic autonomy remains crucial, danger appears in uniting sociality, machines, and environments under the simple and immanent ontological banner of holistic organization. Thus, when Guattari (1989, 142) states that "the ultimate goal of work and human activities in terms of criteria other than those of profit and productivity," it is in line with Pasquinelli's (2015, 1) renewed mandate to think through "the normative autonomy of the subject and its constituent *abnormality*" as *distinct* from those modal properties of institutional and technological forms.[7] The nondiscursive operations of social institutions and machines require their functionality to be recalibrated outside the parameters of economic growth. *Biomorphism* is a useful term to orient this challenging reconsideration. From the ecosystemic fold of ecology and economy, institutional and technological developments that do not directly mimic the automated production of life for the purpose of growth are urgently required. Machines need recalibration toward an autonomous acting capacity that is truly ecological in the sense of technical individuation without capitalist coordinates. From Cooper and Pasquinelli, politics requires an autonomous human subject organizing against the delirious pattern of growth and its deferred limits. Equally, this program calls for room for the potential of social technologies to be articulated outside the easy translation of life into industry, as growth is mistakenly conceived as the equivalent purpose of both organism and machine.

As Philip Mirowski concurs, it is with such sustained conflations of economy and ecology that the shadow of geoengineering responses to climate change appears not as true salvation but as the ultimate backup plan for the eventualities of disaster capitalism: "The neoliberal fallback after the 'cap-and-trade' model inevitably fails will be geoengineering, which derives from the core neoliberal doctrine that entrepreneurs will innovate market solutions to address dire environmental problems" (Mirowski, Walker, and Abboud 2013). The promise of continued economic growth is made in bad faith, carved from a burgeoning financial imagination reconceiving a wrecked Earth as one prospectively terraformed, primed as it is for the continued extraction of surplus. This imaginary is already prototyped, and in the patenting phase, as of Bannon's Biosphere.

Trump's Ecosystem and the Problem of Resilience

Following a highly active hurricane season, CNN ran the headline "Trump Administration Swaps 'Climate Change' for 'Resilience'" (Green 2017). The reporter, Miranda Green, highlights the semiotic shifts that followed the transition from Barack Obama's administration to Trump's environmental policy:

> In the wake of Hurricane Irma, both Federal Emergency Management Agency (FEMA) Administrator Brock Long and acting Homeland Security Secretary Elaine Duke avoided explicitly answering whether the government

needs to be more focused on climate change because of
        hurricanes. Instead, they both said the focus should be on
        resiliency.

Long's response is particularly striking: "*Regardless* of what causes
disasters, it's our job within the Department of Homeland Security
[DHS] and FEMA to manage the consequences. . . . *The only way we
become resilient as a nation is we have to create the true culture of
preparedness among our citizenry*" (Green 2017, emphasis added).
The report continues by tracking a wide range of similar linguistic
slippages occurring throughout various departments developing
environmental perspectives under Trump. Elsewhere, the Natural
Resources Defense Council (NRDC) appeared completely baffled by
Trump's announcement of a $12 billion competition "to increase
resilience to future flood and hurricane disasters," which the NRDC
expert highlighted as "an unexpected proposal" given Trump's
outright antagonism toward climate science: "NRDC has floated a
similar idea with Congress" (Moore 2017). What logic brings Trump
and the NRDC together under the same sign?

Brian Massumi (2009, 155) has excavated Foucault's preliminary
theory of *environmentalité*—environmental governance—within
handwritten manuscript notes from the lectures on *The Birth
of Biopolitics*: "[*Environmentalité*] asserts its own normality, of
crisis: the anywhere, anytime potential for the emergence of the
abnormal. . . . Environmentality as a mode of power is left no
choice but to make do with the abnormally productive 'autonomy.'"
The theory, sketched out on the horizon of Foucault's thinking, is
incomplete at best but proves immensely generative for Massumi's
description of a "war–weather continuum" (158) visible in the
shared and preemptory relationship maintained between the
military preparedness for and neoliberal economic financing of
ecological crisis. This gives a partial explanatory framework for the
interplay between "neoconservative war power" (Massumi 2009,
179) and "disaster capitalism" (Klein 2007) most apparent in George
W. Bush's waffling between Hurricane Katrina as a natural disaster
and as a national economic emergency. Instead,

[Bush] dubbed it a "national *enterprise* emergency." Neo-   **87**
conservatism's naturalization of national security activity
is one half of a double movement. As power moves into
the bare-active realm of emergence to bring life back,
life's induced return is met by an economic expansionism
that wraps life's re-arising into its own global unfolding.
(Massumi 2009, 174)

In response to Hurricane Katrina, Bush redeployed the allegedly
domestic National Guard, recently returned from Iraq, in New
Orleans. The U.S. military, which was legally reserved for foreign
incursion, also circulated throughout Louisiana, collapsing domestic security and foreign invasion within the same local environment.
Again, the ecological/economic management of the interior and
exterior of the household seems at play. With the Pentagon's re-
mapping of civilian and military space came a heinously oppressive
program of economic exploitation in the broad implementation
of what Naomi Klein (2007) has termed the *shock doctrine.* This
doctrine amounts to having free market policies lying in wait for a
crisis opportunity, as crisis etymologically indicates the provoked
need for swift decision and implementation. This strategy plays
out more closely to political elites employing government to
further consolidate power, with the banner of "free market" being
an ideological tool employed in name alone to otherwise secure
profits. Most cynical might be Milton Friedman, aged ninety-three,
who saw Katrina *as an opportunity* to privatize the Louisiana school
system—a process prepared for and completed before most of
New Orleans's poor were able to return to their homes.

As Massumi writes, such events betray a specific strategy to the
emerging form of environmental power that normalizes potential
exposure to state and environmental violence while using those
same conditions to further economize life. Environmental threats
are described as indiscriminate, so the military's response must
be equally ubiquitous and primed like an atmosphere on the
verge of precipitation. "The enterprise aspect of Bush's Katrina
response was represented by his strategy of replacing government

assistance with outsourcing to the private sector and shunning the shelter of government-planned and government-regulated redevelopment for the gale winds of enterprising investment, following eagerly upon those of Katrina" (Massumi 2009, 174). Bush didn't want to return a sense of safety to Louisiana; he wanted to instill a (false) sense of prosperity. Rather than restoration to the homeostatic norms, a new systemic positionality toward the future emerged as the city was reconceived as a resilient one according to the inputs of neoconservative security and neoliberal economics. This is, so far, a familiar reading for how Bush's response to a hurricane melded neoconservative militarism with neoliberal economic strategies. It is more difficult to trace how this doctrine has remained in place through succeeding political administrations.

What makes Massumi's text such a compelling theoretical framework is his insistence that Bush's "national enterprise emergency" was transformed into a fully fledged "*natural* security" (159) for Obama's national security transition team: "the Obama administration's defense of the Bush era rules of exception, which came as a cruel surprise to many hopers, indicates a trans-administration tendency to hold the potential for preemption and its economic coupling in ready reserve" (180). Throughout Massumi's essay, one cannot shake the image of two semiotically distinct yet continuous political regimes—Bush then Obama—reacting to natural and military threats uniformly through the same terms of ubiquitous yet aleatory environmental disruptions. At times, it almost reads as though Massumi describes the state *as an organism*: adapting to a changing external environment through internal renovations (elections, policies, and infrastructure) while retaining the same outward compulsive position toward preparedness for disequilibrium. Is this an example of statecraft responding to the ecosystemic fold of ecology and economy?

It's most clear in Obama's government, I argue, in the translation of the "War on Terror" to what the *Economist* termed in 2014 the "War on Ebola."[8] On October 23, 2014, Craig Spencer returned to New York from Guinea after treating Ebola victims. He contracted the disease and didn't show symptoms for two days, making his way around the city in the time being. Russel Brandom recounts just how totally surveilled Spencer's life was *before* learning he had the disease and how publicly those details traveled after diagnosis to help subdue panic: "Once he was back in New York, nearly everything he did left a trail. There's a reason for the obsessive attention: staying ahead of the virus" (Brandom 2014). A culture of resilience was propagated as an immunitary move: New Yorkers learned every minute detail of Spencer's two days to both assure the population of their public health and prepare them in case of an outbreak.

It is surprisingly easy to switch in a terrorist suspect in the above scenario, as, after all, to find out who Spencer contacted in those two days while moving through the New York public, all the DHS needed to do was interpret data from the already up-and-running post-9/11 security apparatus. Implied is a certain conceptual equivalence of external threat from the perspective of the state, spanning the human (terrorist) and nonhuman (virus). Institutional response to the externality of environmental threat, whether natural or national security, is a functionality maintained from one administration to the next. My reading of the incident is further supported by Obama's 2015 speech on the deployment of the Public Health Service Commissioned Corps to combat Ebola in West Africa:

> Last year, as Ebola spread in West Africa and I said that fighting this disease was more than a national security priority . . . , understand that this corps of public health professionals are on the frontlines all the time. And when you think of some of the most difficult, challenging trag-edies or public health challenges that we've experienced over the last several decades, these are the folks who have been there from the start. After 9/11, after hurri-canes, after Sandy Hook, after Deepwater Horizon or the Boston Marathon bombing, they come in to help support, advise and oftentimes provide direct treatment in some

of the most difficult situations imaginable. . . . They not
        only helped to keep the American people safe; they led a
        global response. (Obama 2015)

Most notable about this speech is the equivalence and conflation
of domestic threats with crises abroad; terrorism with disease,
infrastructural failure, and natural disaster; and international
health with national security. This is not to mention the semiotic re-
inscription of health workers in explicitly militarized terms, or what
the development of "public health infrastructure in many of these
countries" (Obama 2015) might entail in imperial-economic terms.
In the Ebola crisis, the dangers of external threats (environmental
or otherwise) are topologically fed directly inward toward domestic
cultures of preparedness and civic security. As Massumi (2009, 155)
inquires, "What systematicity is this?"

Cooper (2010) has concretely identified this system of governance
as appearing in the ecosystem apparatus. In her study of the
booming market of American investment in weather derivative
financing—second-order speculative futures trading that hedges
environmental risk—she explains how the financing of the
conditions consistent with climate change were first enabled by
Richard Nixon's removal of the gold standard: "We cannot predict
the unfolding of climate change and its effects on prices, even in
the short term. Its parameters of variation are unknowable. Yet
we can create a derivatives contract allowing us to wager on this
very uncertainty. . . . What is at stake in the circulation of capital
today is . . . the event of turbulence itself that becomes tradable"
(178, 179–80). Her broader argument focuses on the magnetic
denomination of debt issuance in global financial markets by the
U.S. dollar—"the world's de facto reserve currency" (168)—and
the accordingly distinct American "privilege of paying its foreign
debts in its own currency" (169) as a topological ordering of "world
imperial power" (181) supported by unrivaled military dominance.
"The problem confronting [centrist American think tank] strategists
is how to navigate the US-dollar denominated world through the
extreme turbulence of financial, climate and energy crisis" (169). By

responding to this problem in strategic planning, in effect, global climate change is viewed as legible according to increasingly volatile conditions of future turbulence marked by uncertain weather as (priceable) environmental risk, uncertain geopolitics rendered as destabilized states (environmental refugees, the testing of critical infrastructure, etc.), and resource scarcity (especially oil depletion). (Nearly beside the point are the new avenues of dethawed access to militarily contested and valuable Arctic territory made increasingly available by global warming.) With turbulent climates of finance and geopolitics looming within the strategic planning of economic and military policy, Cooper charts designs being drawn up not only to *survive* the turbulence but to profit and securitize in its wake. This logical position toward the future perversely underwrites the continued manufacture of said turbulent conditions by maintaining fossil fuel–based growth economies. Then, the integrated response to the reticulation of future financial, ecological, and energy crisis assumes that

> turbulence cannot be averted then. . . . Rather the aim will be that of maintaining the topological cohesion of a world in and through the most extreme periods of turbulence. In complex systems theory, this property of topological cohesion is referred to as "resilience" (the term, which was first used in its contemporary scientific understanding in ecosystems theory, is now ubiquitous in strategic thinking). (183)

The shift to resilience relies on the hedge against serious global warming mitigation or climate stabilization. For Cooper, resilience is the working strategy to strengthen American national security (neoconservatism) and economic dominance (neoliberalism) through impending crises while maintaining the topology of American geopolitical supremacy defined along the axes of debt imperialism and military strength. By pivoting toward a future-oriented system best suited to take advantage of inbound turbulent conditions, material acts in prevention are functionally discouraged.

In a subsequent study, Cooper and Jeremy Walker have described in depth the genealogy of resilience that, unsurprisingly, follows from the ecosystem apparatus. They highlight the symmetry between ecologist C. S. Holling and his introduction of complexity science to ecosystem theory, with the late neoliberal economic philosophy of Friedrich Hayek. Cooper and Walker (2012, 145–46) illustrate the disunity-in-unity characterizing the conceptual application of complexity to economy and ecology as such:

> The key image of science that propelled the formalisation of economics (in the 1870s) and ecology (in the 1950s), was of smooth and continuous returns to equilibrium after shock, an image derived from different vintages of mechanics and thermodynamics. Holling's widely cited paper "Resilience and Stability of Ecological Systems" (1973) represents the destabilisation of the notion of "equilibrium" as the core of the ecosystem concept and the normal terminus of ecosystem trajectory. . . . What Holling seeks to define instead, is a complex notion of resilience which can account for the ability of an ecosystem to remain cohesive even while undergoing extreme perturbations. If stability refers to the familiar notion of a return to equilibrium, "ecological" resilience designates the complex biotic interactions that determine "the persistence of relationships within a system," thus resilience is "a measure of the ability of these systems to absorb changes of state variables . . . and still persist."

Cooper and Walker proceed by mapping how Holling's concepts guide environmental policy development in several prominent think tanks, most notably the Resilience Alliance. Holling's later ecological theories transition toward figuring capital accumulation away from linear models of political economy and into the "crisis tendencies of complex adaptive systems" (147) giving foundation for resource management theories advocating the financing, securitizing, and militarization of the biosphere. While Holling and Hayek did not cite one another, the two have structural similarities

in their respective citations and rhetorical embrace of complex
systems theory. Walker and Cooper imply a mutual conceptual
foundation, which is by now familiar to the disunity-in-unity strategies of the cybernetic apparatus and its ecosystemic by-product.

Intuitively, Massumi's question—what systematicity is this?—
suggests a common logic preempting a future defined by an
increasingly turbulent set of atmospheric, financial, and insurgent
conditions, which appears satisfied by Cooper and Walker's
description of resilience. Resilience policies semiotically absorb the
concerns of varied administrations, including Bush's consolidation
of FEMA and the EPA under the guidance of the Department of
Homeland Security's 2007 mandate to use natural disasters "as
opportunities for the selective transformation of urban space"
(Cooper and Walker 2012, 154). Or, resilience is visible in the
Obama administration's couching of Deepwater Horizon in terms
of a terrorist attack, wherein the linguistic shifts along the war–
weather continuum serve to justify the unavoidable dependence
of the security state upon the petrochemical industry (and its
reserves) to fuel its war machine both domestically and abroad
(McClintock 2012, 4). In words that portend the Trump administration's call for a "true culture of preparedness among our citizenry"
(Green 2017), Cooper and Walker (2012, 155) discern in resilience a
"general systems theory of 'socio-ecological governance'" forming
a completely normalized sensibility oriented toward maintaining
multidynamic stability as though a coherent program of civic
defense: "Within this optic, preparedness would seem to demand
the generic ability to adapt to unknowable contingencies rather
than actual prevention or indeed adaptation to future events of
known probability" (153). Correspondingly, they continue, Hayek's
late theories posit the equivalence of catastrophes "(natural, social
or economic)" as an inevitable failure inherent to the limits of
socialized management and control, as though catastrophe is the
teleological consequence of governmental intervention (Cooper
and Walker 2012, 154). Then, from Hayek's perspective, this means
that the failure to mitigate climate change is not itself the problem.

Instead, Cooper and Walker see in Hayek's resilience theory an economic philosophy with contempt for political strategies of social governance: "what is called for instead is a 'culture' of resilience that turns crisis response into a strategy of permanent, open-ended responsiveness, integrating emergency preparedness into the infrastructures of everyday life and the psychology of citizens" (153–54). These are nearly the same terms adopted by Trump's FEMA. Within this optic, addressing climate change is not about moving society off oil, as there is no society. Cultures of resilience provide an alternate solution. From the perspective of resilience, it's about deregulation and encouraging individuals toward cultures of disaster preparation.

As in the integrated whole of the organicist state and Guattari's three ecologies, ecological resilience and its prepared security infrastructure imagines its environmental subjects as a "culture" in the bacterial sense: growth from a nourishing medium that rhetorically enlists the agency of the full political spectrum. An allegedly environmentalist program, resilience proves deeply neoliberal in its discount of mitigation strategies. Individuals are positioned as ecosystemic effects without any autonomous potential to re-form environmental relations outside the twinned concerns of national security and petrochemical industrial growth, otherwise, ecology and economy. Collectivity is effectively written out in advance by the preemptory position seeking to maintain cohesive adaptation of individual survivors during inbound turbulence.

It would be irresponsible to discuss resilience without pointing to the deep strain of eugenics that the discourse cultivates, especially with regard to climate migration and refugees. Resilience "reiterates and modifies the Darwinian law of natural selection" by recalibrating social norms toward the turbulent conditions of nonequilibrium: "in this context, the appeal to ecological security is often invoked as a means of distinguishing those who are sufficiently resilient to survive as dignified participants in a globally integrated world from those who are either too resilient or not resilient enough" (Cooper and Walker 2012, 156). Orit Halpern, in

parsing the 2012 ideology of "Fix and Fortify" in New York City fol- **95**
lowing Hurricane Sandy, identifies how the phrase both abstracts
the source of violence (industrial capitalism) and cultivates a sense
of civic "resilient hope" for urban renewal, all while encouraging
belief in the "continue[d] myths of economic and technical growth
while embracing a future understood as finite and catastrophic"
(Halpern, Mitchell, and Geoghegan 2017). This draws into sharp
relief the racist logic running through the gentrification prospects
of resilience operations at scale: "planned obsolescence and
preemptive destruction combine here to encourage the introduction of more computation into the environment—and emphasize
as well that resilience of the human species may necessitate
the sacrifice of 'suboptimal' populations" (Halpern, Mitchell, and
Geoghegan 2017, 123). In all the technofantasy architectural
mock-ups of floating smart cities adapting to climate change, there
remain the hidden labor conditions and the unequal allocation of
scarce materials further exposing those historically placed at risk,
as obscured sacrifices are made for the tradable, "sustainable," and
survivable future. All the while, Exxon builds oil rigs to adjust to rising seas (Lieberman and Rust 2015). Precisely what Guattari meant
by Donald Trump's algaeic proliferation, and the cultures it seeks
to grow, can be learned by following resilience as one significant
consequence of the twentieth-century ecosystem project.

||||||||||||||||||||

Nicole Shukin (2016, 3) recently put it succinctly: "Resilience is
exploited as a resource of flexible labor and life accustomed to
the chronically precarious conditions of unlimited growth." This
chapter began by outlining the promise of Pasquinelli's recommendation for a renewed study of Guattari's "*machinic ecology*" seeking
to repair labor's abstraction into information and energy expedited
by the twentieth century's technoscientific projects. As outlined
here, this process is highly visible in charting the history and
operationality of the concept of the ecosystem: from theory of the
mind through to resilience policies. By locating the discourse of the
ecosystem within longer philosophical conversations surrounding

the relationship between organic unity and normative potentiality, the proximity of the ecosystem to theories of organicism is better understood for its full political implications: "the perception of the whole earth as ecosystem (as in the Gaia hypothesis)" (Pasquinelli 2017, 320) requires a critique of political economy.

Not unlike the "recursive irony" defining the technonatural hybridity of the ecosystem, to use Bryant's (2006) phrase, Pasquinelli (2017) implies it is more than a coincidence that the outcome of the industrial division of energy and information as an abstraction of labor is climate change driven by accelerated capitalism, as global warming is made visible by the same epistemological tools that power the problem. Such is the recursive trap of planetary computation:

> With almost identical techniques, global data centers accumulate information and intelligence, not just about the world's climate but also about financial markets, logistical chains, international terrorism, and, more importantly, social networks of billions of individuals. Is the similarity of climate science and control apparatuses just a coincidence, or does it point to a more general form of governance? The vast network of climate science appears like an extended cybernetic loop with big institutions taking the role of the nervous system of a pretty large organism—planet earth. (320)

Pasquinelli's provocation here regarding large-scale forms of environmental governance is important and, as highlighted earlier, in line with a longer set of historical transactions that can be traced through to questions placing the organic individual in relation to the social and technological whole. Indeed, as the history of the ecosystem shows, this form of governance is already identifiable in policy as resilience.

Yet, there is still the problem of the ecosystem as fashioned by economy and ecology. As prophetic as Guattari's text appears while regarding his admittedly uncanny forecasting of Donald Trump's invasive ecology, Pasquinelli's (2017, 321) insistence on reuniting "the civilizations of Silicon and Carbon, the lineages of Information and Energy" as the *"carbosilicon machine,"* requires additional commentary, especially as he maintains that "it may be better to try and consolidate the assemblage of energy and information into new systemic notions." I find his position *toward* new systems intriguing, given the emphasis on "autonomy" as articulated across both of his arguments reviewed here: normative social auton-omy as "self-governing and able to invent new laws, rules, and habits. . . . To rethink social autonomy today one has to see what the autonomy of energy and the autonomy of information mean together in an expanded (and technified) notion of labor" (323). This proposition is certainly in line with Guattari's programmatic for collective management and control of the three ecologies, as steered away from profit and productivity. However, I draw this point out in caution because, given the danger of holism, I believe renewed focus on the assumed progressiveness of the system needs qualification.

Resilience proves a particularly thorny concept. As Cooper and Walker (2012, 157) demonstrate, referencing the influence of complex systems theory on social science, it is the complex social system itself that "thrives upon disruptions to its own state of equilibrium. . . . By metabolizing critique into its internal dynamic, the complex adaptive system remains self-referential even when it encounters the most violent of shocks." The risk, here, is that adaptive complex systems are defiant to critique insofar as commentators who employ "the system they set out to challenge" ultimately find their challenge self-referential and systemically enclosed, effectively cannibalized. The target of criticism "reabsor-b[s] critique into the workings of systems theory itself" (Cooper and Walker 2012, 157). This is best illustrated by the easy movement of Holling's resilient ecosystem from a position of ecological critique to paradigmatic complicity with neoliberal finance, neoconservative militarization, and environmental governance. Cooper and Walker stress that to confront a system that "transform[s] perturbation into an endogenous feature of the system [a]s a catalyst to further self-differentiation" (157), what is required are "completely different terms" and "a movement of thought that is truly counter-systemic" (157). Guattari's ecological theory—its celebrated utility, inspiration, and prescience—needs to be carefully considered in this cautionary regard, given *The Three Ecologies*'s reluctant embrace of cybernetic systems and the immanent critique they afford. Then, at the limit of the problem of resilience is the imperative for flights of thought beyond the system.

As Pasquinelli (2017, 321) reminds us, the "incestuous relation between planetary control and planetary disequilibrium" is a complication located in the abstraction between "civilizations of Silicon and Carbon." His emphasis on historically repairing the separation of energy and information as they bear on contemporary political formations is crucial, and the forms of struggle the implied historical cleavage might call for remain a site for future study. As I have illustrated here, the ecosystem is one such chimeric concept that provides a platform with which to describe and test the appositeness of existing socioecological theories. Insofar as it provides a common ground upon which economy and ecology do play, the ecosystem concept remains a productive term of media in its conceptual relay of energy and information; ecology and economy; and its description of the recursive epistemological lens of the system that nests environment, technology, and mind.

To close, Cooper (2008, 20) argues while regarding the "bioeconomy" that the "capitalist delirium" driving the repeated reinvention of the limits to growth follows from Freud: "the psychotic delirium, as opposed to the neurotic fantasy, is crucially concerned with the breakdown and recreation of whole worlds. Delirium is systemic, not representative. It seeks to refashion the world rather than interpret it." Then, as with Tansley's grafting of psychoanalysis, the ecosystem is perhaps best viewed as one such delirious mechanism recursively derived from an underlining systemic logic: ecosystem as a cognitive machine raising and destroying worlds with the privileged machination of shuffling and sorting the reticulation of the psyche, environment, and technology between the poles of economic growth and the promise of renewable life. It is equally important to recall that Tansley formed the ecosystem with specific reference to its environmental negativity—a constitutional absence that the concept itself is driven toward. Exploring this forgotten exterior to the ecosystem might prove rewarding as we chart steps outside the ecology of mind.

Notes

1   I would like to express my gratitude to Wendy Hui Kyong Chun, Derek Woods, and Florian Sprenger for their invaluable feedback and vital commentary in responding to drafts of this chapter.

2   Donna Haraway highlighted the "ecosystem" as a primary example of the hybrid cybernetic organism, or cyborg, figuration in both "A Cyborg Manifesto" (Haraway 1991) and *Modest_Witness*: "the cyborg live[s] without innocence in the regime of technobiopower, where literacy is about the joining of informatics, biologics, and economics—about the kinship of the . . . ecosystem" (Haraway 1997, 2).

3   For more on the Cold War militarized context driving the Odums' conceptual development of the cybernetic ecosystem, see Laura Martin's (2018) "Proving Grounds: Ecological Fieldwork in the Pacific and the Materialization of Ecosystems."

4   Besides Anker's account, see Sagan (1991), Luke (1995), Bryant (2006), and Steyerl (2017). See also Sagan and Margulis's (1989) publication *Biospheres: From Earth to Space,* where they make the case for extraterrestrial technoecological biospheres as self-regulating colonies.

5   I am grateful to Lukas Rieppel for pointing me toward Bannon's work on Biosphere 2 and how this ideology contradicts the "no lifeboats" argument.

6   Hito Steyerl has initiated a conversation about Bannon's administration of Biosphere II as "a great metaphor for technofascism" (Steyerl and Vidokle 2017).

7   Henning Schmidgen (2005) also sees this distinction as made by Canguilhem in 1952. Schmidgen locates the careful distinction between the mode of existence of organic and technical objects as an early critical response to American cybernetics, and it is worth pointing out that this position on the potential "organology" (Hörl 2015, 4) of institutions and technology deeply influenced another of Canguilhem's students, Gilbert Simondon, who made a sustained point about the distinct evolutionary patterns of organic and technical individuals.

8   For more on this analogy, see also Karen Greenberg's (2014) perspective.

References

Agamben, Giorgio. 2009. *"What Is an Apparatus?" and Other Essays.* Stanford, Calif.: Stanford University Press.

Anker, Peder. 2017. "Ouroboros Architecture." In *The Routledge Companion to Biology in Art and Architecture, 112–35.* New York: Routledge.

Bateson, Gregory. 1972. *Steps to an Ecology of Mind: Collected Essays in Anthropology, Psychiatry, Evolution, and Epistemology.* Chicago: University of Chicago Press.

Bowker, Geof. 1993. "How to Be Universal: Some Cybernetic Strategies, 1943–70." *Social Studies of Science* 23, no. 1: 107–27.

Brandom, Russell. 2014. "The NYC Ebola Patient Has Turned Us All into Spies." *The Verge,* October 24.

Bryant, William Harold. 2006. "Whole System, Whole Earth: The Convergence of Technology and Ecology in Twentieth-Century American Culture." PhD diss., University of Iowa.

Cameron, Laura. 2004. "Ecosystem." In *Patterned Ground: Entanglements of Nature and Culture,* edited by Stephan Harrison, Steve Pile, and Nigel Thrift, 55–57. London: Reaktion.

Cameron, Laura, and Sinead Earley. 2015. "The Ecosystem—Movements, Connections, Tensions and Translations." *Geoforum* 65: 473–81.

Canguilhem, Georges. 1943. *Essai sur quelques problèmes concernant le normal et le pathologique.* Publications de la faculté des lettres de l'université de strasbourg 100. Clermont-Ferrand: Impr. la Montagne.

Canguilhem, Georges. (1952) 2008. "Machine and Organism." In *Knowledge of Life,* 75–97. Bronx, N.Y.: Fordham University Press.

Canguilhem, Georges. (1966) 1991. *The Normal and the Pathological.* New York: Zone Books.

Carson, Rachel. (1962) 2002. *Silent Spring.* Boston: Houghton Mifflin.

Chakrabarty, Dipesh. 2009. "The Climate of History: Four Theses." *Critical Inquiry* 35, no. 2: 197–222.

Commoner, Barry. 1972. *The Closing Circle: Confronting Environmental Crisis.* London: Cape.

Cooper, Melinda. 2008. *Life as Surplus: Biotechnology and Capitalism in the Neoliberal Era.* Seattle: University of Washington Press.

Cooper, Melinda. 2010. "Turbulent Worlds: Financial Markets and Environmental Crisis." *Theory, Culture, and Society* 27, no. 2–3: 167–90.

Cooper, Melinda, and Jeremy Walker. 2012. "Genealogies of Resilience: From Systems Ecology to the Political Economy of Crisis Adaptation." *Security Dialogue* 42, no. 2: 143–60.

Deleuze, Gilles. (1989) 1995. "What Is a *Dispositif?*" In *Two Regimes of Madness: Texts and Interviews 1975–1995,* 338–48. Los Angeles, Calif.: Semiotext(e).

Deleuze, Gilles. (1990) 1995. "Postscript on Control Societies." In *Negotiations, 1972–1995,* 177–82. Los Angeles, Calif.: Semiotext(e).

Deleuze, Gilles, and Félix Guattari. (1980) 1987. *A Thousand Plateaus: Capitalism and Schizophrenia.* Minneapolis: University of Minnesota Press.

Edwards, Paul. 2012. "Entangled Histories: Climate Science and Nuclear Weapons Research." *Bulletin of the Atomic Scientists* 68, no. 4: 28–40.

Ehrlich, Paul. 1968. *The Population Bomb.* New York: Ballantine Books.

Foster, John Bellamy. 1999. "Marx's Theory of Metabolic Rift: Classical Foundations for Environmental Sociology." *American Journal of Sociology* 105, no. 2: 366–405.

Foucault, Michel. 1977. *Discipline and Punish: Birth of the Prison.* New York: Pantheon Books.

Foucault, Michel. 1978. *The History of Sexuality.* New York: Pantheon Books.

Foucault, Michel. 1980. *Power/Knowledge: Selected Interviews and Other Writings 1972–1977.* Edited by Colin Gordon. New York: Pantheon.

Foucault, Michel. 2004. *The Birth of Biopolitics: Lectures at the Collège de France 1978–1979.* New York: Palgrave Macmillan.

Gabrys, Jennifer. 2013. *Digital Rubbish: A Natural History of Electronics.* Ann Arbor: University of Michigan Press.

Gardner, Timothy. 2018. "Trump Nominates Coal, Nuclear Bailout Supporter to U.S. Power Agency." Reuters, October 3.

Garfield, Leanna. 2017. "Trump Says He Wants a Solar Border Wall—Here's How Many Homes It Could Power." *Business Insider,* July 13.

Geoghegan, Bernard Dionysius. 2011. "From Information Theory to French Theory: Jakobson, Lévi-Strauss, and the Cybernetic Apparatus." *Critical Inquiry* 38 (Autumn): 96–126.

Golley, Frank Benjamin. 1993. *A History of the Ecosystem Concept in Ecology: More Than the Sum of Its Parts.* New Haven, Conn.: Yale University Press.

Green, Miranda. 2017. "Trump Administration Swaps 'Climate Change' for 'Resilience.'" CNN, September 30.

Green, Miranda. 2018. "Zinke Cites 'Environmental Disaster' in Sending Park Police to Border." *Hill,* June 3.

Greenberg, Karen. 2014. "America's Response to Ebola Looks Disturbingly Similar to the War on Terror." *Mother Jones,* November 12.

Guattari, Félix. 1989. "The Three Ecologies." *new formations* 8 (Summer): 131–47.

Halpern, Orit. 2017. "Hopeful Resilience." *e-flux Architecture,* April 19.

Halpern, Orit, Robert Mitchell, and Bernard Dionysius Geoghegan. 2017. "The Smartness Mandate: Notes toward a Critique." *Grey Room* 68 (Summer): 106–29.

Haraway, Donna. 1991. "A Cyborg Manifesto: Science, Technology and Socialist-Feminism in the Late Twentieth Century." In *Simians, Cyborgs, and Women: The Reinvention of Nature,* 149–81. New York: Routledge.

Haraway, Donna. 1997. *Modest_Witness@Second_Millenium: FemaleMan_Meets_Onco-Mouse: Feminism and Technoscience.* New York: Routledge.

Hiltzik, Michael. 2017. "A New Study Shows How Exxon Mobil Downplayed Climate Change When It Knew the Problem Was Real." *Los Angeles Times,* August 22.

Hörl, Erich. 2013. "A Thousand Ecologies: The Process of Cyberneticization and General Ecology." In *The Whole Earth: California and the Disappearance of the Outside,* 121–30. New York: Sternberg Press.

Hörl, Erich. 2015. "The Technological Condition." *Parrhesia* 22: 1–15.

Jerving, Sara, Katie Jennings, Masako Melissa Hirsch, and Susanne Rust. 2015. "What Exxon Knew about the Earth's Melting Arctic." *Los Angeles Times,* October 9.

Klein, Naomi. 2007. *The Shock Doctrine: The Rise of Disaster Capitalism.* Toronto: Alfred A. Knopf.

Klein, Naomi. 2017. "I did an edit: With Irma and Harvey, Carbon Cuts + Tax Hikes on the rich needed more than ever to pay for devastation + the cost of denial." Twitter, September 13. https://twitter.com/naomiaklein/status/907959080572010497.

Lafontaine, Céline. 2007. "The Cybernetic Matrix of 'French Theory.'" *Theory, Culture, and Society* 24, no. 5: 27–46.

Lieberman, Amy, and Susanne Rust. 2015. "Big Oil Braced for Global Warming While It Fought Regulations." *Los Angeles Times,* December 31.

Lovelock, James. 1995. *Gaia: A New Look at Life on Earth.* Oxford: Oxford University Press.

Luke, Timothy. 1995. "Reproducing Planet Earth? The Hubris of Biosphere 2." *Ecologist* 25, no. 4: 157–62.

Martin, Laura. 2018. "Proving Grounds: Ecological Fieldwork in the Pacific and the Materialization of Ecosystems." *Environmental History* 23: 567–92.

Martin, Reinhold. 2004. "Environment, c. 1973." *Grey Room* 14 (Winter): 78–101.

Masco, Joseph. 2010. "Bad Weather: On Planetary Crisis." *Social Studies of Science* 40, no. 1: 7–40.

Masco, Joseph. 2017. "The Crisis in Crisis." *Current Anthropology* 58, no. 15: S65–76.

Massumi, Brian. 2009. "National Enterprise Emergency: Steps toward an Ecology of Powers." *Theory, Culture, and Society* 26, no. 6: 153–85.

McClintock, Anne. 2012. "Slow Violence and the BP Oil Crisis in the Gulf of Mexico: Militarizing Environmental Catastrophe." *Hemispheric Institute E-Misférica* 9.1–9.2.

Meadows, Donella H., et al. 1972. *The Limits to Growth: A Report for the Club of Rome's Project on the Predicament of Mankind.* New York: Universe Books.

Meadows, Donella H., et al. 1992. *Beyond the Limits: Global Collapse or a Sustainable Future.* London: Earthscan.

Meiklejohn, Brad. 2017. "Under Cover of Tax Bill, Congress Gives Away the Arctic National Wildlife Refuge—to Drillers." *Los Angeles Times,* December 22.

Mirowski, Philip. 2013. "The Neoliberal Response to Global Warming." In *Never Let a Good Crisis Go to Waste,* 334–42. New York: Verso.

Mirowski, Philip, Jeremy Walker, and Antoinette Abboud. 2013. "Beyond Denial." *Overland* 210 (Autumn). https://overland.org.au/previous-issues/issue-210/feature-philip-mirowski-jeremy-walker-antoinette-abboud/.

Moore, Rob. 2017. "Trump Announced a $12 Billion Resilience Competition??" NRDC, November 21. https://www.nrdc.org/experts/rob-moore/trump-announced-12-billion-resilience-competition.

Natter, Ari, and Mark Chedia. 2017. "Trump Hands $3.7 Billion Lifeline to Last U.S. Nuke Project." *Bloomberg Markets,* September 29.

Niiler, Eric. 2016. "Trump's Chief Strategist Steve Bannon Ran a Massive Climate Experiment." *Wired,* December 7.

Obama, Barack. 2015. "President Obama Meeting with Public Health Officials." C-SPAN, September 25. https://www.c-span.org/video/?328326-3/president-obama-meeting-public-health-officials.

Parenti, Christian. 2011. "American Walls and Demagogues." In *Tropic of Chaos: Climate Change and the New Geography of Violence*, 207–24. New York: Nation Books.

Pasquinelli, Matteo. 2015. "What an Apparatus Is Not: On the Archeology of the Norm in Foucault, Canguilhem, and Goldstein." *Parrhesia Journal* 22 (May): 79–89.

Pasquinelli, Matteo. 2017. "The Automaton of the Anthropocene: On Carbosilicon Machines and Cyberfossil Capital." *South Atlantic Quarterly* 116, no. 2: 311–26.

Sagan, Dorion. 1991. *Biospheres: The Metamorphosis of Planet Earth*. New York: McGraw-Hill.

Sagan, Dorion, and Lynn Margulis. 1989. *Biospheres from Earth to Space*. Hillside, N.J.: Enslow.

Schmidgen, Henning. 2005. "Thinking Technological and Biological Beings: Gilbert Simondon's Philosophy of Machines." *Revista do Departamento de Psicologia* 17, no. 2: 11–18.

Shukin, Nicole. 2016. "The Biocapital of Living—and the Art of Dying—after Fukushima." *Postmodern Culture* 26, no. 2.

Steyerl, Hito, and Anton Vidokle. 2017. "Cosmic Catwalk and the Production of Time." *e-flux Architecture* 82 (May). https://www.e-flux.com/journal/82/134989/cosmic-catwalk-and-the-production-of-time/.

Stiegler, Bernard, with Anaïs Nony. 2015. "Bernard Stiegler on Automatic Society." *Third Rail* 5: 16–17.

Tansley, A. G. 1935. "The Use and Abuse of Vegetational Concepts and Terms." *Ecology* 16: 284–307.

Turner, Fred. 2006. *From Counterculture to Cyberculture: Stewart Brand, the Whole Earth Network, and the Rise of Digital Utopianism*. Chicago: University of Chicago Press.

Turner, Fred. 2010. "The Politics of the Whole circa 1968—and Now." In *The Whole Earth: California and the Disappearance of the Outside*, 43–48. New York: Sternberg Press.

Authors

Gertrud Koch is senior professor at the Freie Universität Berlin and visiting professor at Brown University. She is the author of numerous books. Her last publication in English was *Breaking Bad, Breaking Out, Breaking Even* and in German was *Die Wiederkehr der Illusion.*

Thomas Pringle is an SSHRC doctoral and presidential fellow at Brown University, where he is a PhD candidate in the Department of Modern Culture and Media.

Bernard Stiegler is head of the Institut de recherche et d'innovation du Centre Pompidou and president of the Ars Industrialis association. He is the author of more than thirty books, including the recent English translation of *Automatic Society: The Future of Work.*